"Amazing transformation happens when an ordinary church—a community of faith—prays and obeys the call of God to reach out to a highly resistant people group. This is a powerful story about prayer, by faithful men and women who have chosen to pray for and work among a challenging people, for the sake of Christ. Read this book and pass it on to your church leadership."

—Harold Britton, Director of Church–Missionary Relationships at WorldVenture

One of the greatest faith building times we can have is when we're in the midst of ministry that is so hard, so impossible, so discouraging, that we know that whatever positive happens it absolutely must be the Lord doing it. That's the story of THE PRAYERS OF MANY. Men, women and children from all over the world, pleading with God to do something and then watching in amazement as He does it His way.

— Gene Kissinger, long-time Pastor at Cherry Hills Community Church

God's heartbeat for the nations, for the unreached, and for every tribe is something I'm confident we'll never understand this side of heaven. Yet, D.G. Wynn has caught a glimpse of that much greater than most ever do. In this book she captures stories of real people whose heroic actions will reawaken your soul. Whether you're looking to learn about a specific people, or in search of stories that will defibrillate your heart, look no further!

—Shane Farmer, Senior Pastor, Cherry Hills Community Church

THE PRAYERS OF MANY

THE STORY OF A CHURCH ON MISSION

Dear Diane
& Ken,

Thank you
for your help!
Pray hard.

THE PRAYERS OF MANY

THE STORY OF A CHURCH ON MISSION

By

D.G. Wynn

An imprint of Armory Publishing Group, LLC
www.ArmoryPublishing.com

The Prayers of Many: The Story of a Church On Mission
by D.G. Wynn

ISBN 978-0-9963869-6-8 (paperback)
ISBN 978-0-9963869-7-5 (ebook, MOBI version)
ISBN 978-0-9963869-8-2 (ebook, EPUB version)

Published by Armory Press, an imprint of the Armory Publishing Group, LLC.
P.O. Box 13, Littleton, CO 80160-0013.
www.armorypublishing.com

Editing provided by Andrew Sloan
Interior Design by Julia Evans
Cover Design by The Verbosity Co.

Library of Congress Control Number: 2016932261
Publisher's Cataloging-in-Publication data

Names: Wynn, D.G., author.
Title: The Prayers of many : the story of a church on mission / D.G. Wynn.
Identifiers: ISBN 978-0-9963869-6-8 (pbk.) | 978-0-9963869-7-5 (ebook). | LCCN 2016932261.
Description: Includes bibliographical references. | Denver [Colorado] : Armory Press, an imprint of Armory Publishing Group, LLC, 2016.
Subjects: LCSH Prayer--Christianity. | Christian life. | Missions. | BISAC RELIGION/ Christian Life/Prayer. | RELIGION/Christian Ministry/Missions. | RELIGION/Prayer. Classification: LCC BV213 .W96 2016 | DDC 248/.3–dc23

TABLE OF CONTENTS

To all the faithful men and women who contribute to spreading the gospel in the hard-to-reach places of the world. And, to CHCC and Pastor G. for their faithfulness.

DISCLAIMER

For the safety of all those involved, details about the people and their province are purposely vague to stifle the ease of guessing who and where they are. The names of all past and present missionaries, brave mission organizations trying to make headway on behalf of the gospel, the home team and short-term team members have been changed for their protection. Obscuring their names is vital, but equally important is altering the names of those with whom they work, because the work *is still happening* at this very moment.

While pseudonyms are used, all the people mentioned are real people, with real stories, who are really laying down their lives on behalf of the Kingdom in an effort to bring the love of Jesus and His epic gift of salvation to an unreached people group somewhere in the world. If you are inspired by their stories, even if it is with their pseudonym, pray for them. God knows their name.

The scope of this book is not as expansive as the real story. It can't be. This story is too big for one book. As a result, some people and events were chosen to share a glimpse of the whole work being done. However, for each story told, there are decades of stories that go untold. While there are major and minor characters in the book, every real-life person who has given even an ounce of effort to help bring the gospel to the Chantik is a significant person, and we pray the Lord blesses them for their contribution.

ONE

It's Time to Pray

The prayer of a righteous person is powerful and effective.

~James 5:16b (NIV)

At some point or another we've all wanted to see real change in the world, but many of us—too many—have stopped believing it's possible. To believe in world change, in this modern and cynical era, is akin to believing in the Tooth Fairy. Skeptics look at your hope and throw words at you like daggers—*Pollyanna, Idealist, Do-gooder*—and dismiss you in the same breath. And yet, changing the world isn't just the far-fetched longing of an idealist. It should be the rally cry for every believer in Jesus Christ. The fact is that if the prayer of one righteous person is powerful and effective, then the prayers of many should change the world. But you should know, this isn't a book about how to pray. It's a book about what happens *when* we pray.

In order to believe that world change is possible we need to reclaim our belief in prayer as a powerful weapon against the apathy of believing that the world is lost to Satan's malicious whims and to man's selfish and destructive tendencies. Every time we seek the Lord in prayer we are claiming and reclaiming our belief that our great God is the Ultimate Ruler over this world. We affirm His reign now and forever on His throne. But that raises an additional problem,

doesn't it? Many of us need to be reminded that prayer is effective—
that *God answers prayers.*

Regardless of *how* He answers our prayers—yes, no, or wait—think
of the parable of the persistent widow in Luke 18:1-8. Jesus shares this
parable to illustrate how important it
is to pray *without giving up* and that
faith is vital in the prayer process.
Hebrews 11:1 reminds us that "faith
is confidence in what we hope
for and assurance about what we do
not see" (NIV). And Lamentations
3:25-26 joins that chorus by adding,
"The LORD is good to those whose

> ## Pursuing the Lord together, particularly in prayer, is a vital part of living in the Kingdom of God.

hope is in him, to the one who seeks him; it is good to wait quietly
for the salvation of the LORD" (NIV). Our challenge is to be persistent,
faith-filled, and patient in our prayers. It's not easy, but it is possible.

One Plus One Equals More Than Two

So how do we do it? How do we live out that epic life of prayer that
all of us wannabe world changers desire? We start by doing some
eternal math.

The Lord promises us that where two or more are gathered in
His name, He is there with them also.[1] That means when He adds
His infinite presence to our finite numbers, we wind up with so very
much more than what we started with. What would it even look like
to be *more than* powerful, *more than* effective in prayer?

Pursuing the Lord together, particularly in prayer, is a vital part of
living in the Kingdom of God. It gives us the opportunity to shoulder
each other's burdens, celebrate victories, build one another up, and
advance the Kingdom by asking for the Lord's will to be done here

on earth as it is in heaven.[2] And when we gather together and pray with purpose—arming ourselves for spiritual battle, putting the King of Kings at the fore of each small band of prayer warriors—the principalities tremble.

One Call For All

As believers, we are personal witnesses of His glory, love, grace, and mercy in our lives; and as much as we personally need all that (and more) from God, we need to want it that desperately for others. Every believer has an individual call on their life, but beyond that every believer also has a universal call for which they are responsible: *to seek and save the lost*. This responsibility finds its precedent in Christ, wherein Luke 19:10 clearly states, "For the Son of Man came to seek and to save the lost" (NIV). And, since we are to strive to be Christ-like, it follows that this grand purpose is our privilege and mandate as well.

Being mindful of the task at hand, it is imperative to understand the scope of the undertaking we have before us. According to the Joshua Project in 2015, there are nearly 17,000 people groups who exist on earth.[3] Just over 7,000 of those people groups are considered unreached.[4] "From the viewpoint of evangelization, a 'people group' is the largest possible group within which the gospel can spread as a discipling, or church planting movement without encountering barriers of understanding or acceptance."[5] And, to be an *unreached people group* requires that it be "a people group within which there is no indigenous community of believing Christians able to evangelize this people group."[6] That is the scope of our task: 7,000 unreached people groups in both the nearest and furthest corners of the world have yet to hear the Good News of the gospel of Jesus Christ in any significant way that would allow for an indigenous church body to exist and spread.

Those sobering numbers should confirm the mandate and spur us to further prayer and action. Personal prayer has any number of motivations; however, when we pray together as one church, one body, it should regularly be to one end—salvation of the lost— because with salvation comes every other good thing: justice, mercy, peace, and more.

One Church, One People, Many Prayers

Prayer is, and has always been, an open invitation to the body of Christ to participate in the movement of God in the world. To connect with Him. To listen and learn to hear His voice. To know His heart more fully and to follow Him further into His will for ourselves and for the nations.

The following chapters tell the story of God sparking a prayer movement in one church on behalf of one people. In His sovereignty and generosity, He wove countless individuals, churches, organizations, and mission agencies into His greater effort. However, *this* story is told through the lens of one church, Cherry Hills Community Church (CHCC), and its twenty-five-year commitment to sharing the gospel with an unreached people group referred to as the *Chantik*.

Though the intensity of effort came in waves, twenty-five years later the pages of this book relay dozens and dozens of specific prayers that have been answered in part, in full, or for a time. This story represents every church and every believer who dedicates themselves in prayer to participate in the Lord's heart for the nations. It walks the path the church traveled to reach the Chantik and illustrates how vital prayer was throughout the journey. This is what it looks like when God answers the prayers of His church to change the world.

Chapter 1 Citations

1. Holy Bible. New International Version. Matthew 18:20.
2. Holy Bible. New International Version. Matthew 6:10.
3. "All People Groups by Country." Joshua Project. Accessed January 28, 2015. http://joshuaproject.net/resources/datasets.
4. "Only Unreached People Groups by Country." Joshua Project. Accessed January 28, 2015. http://joshuaproject.net/resources/datasets.
5. Steven C. Hawthorne, "Mandate on the Mountain," in *Perspectives on the World Christian Movement* (2014, 4th ed.).
6. R. D. Winter and B. D. Koch, "Finishing the Task," in R. D. Winter and S. C. Hawthorne (eds.), *Perspectives on the World Christian Movement: A Reader* (4th ed.). Pasadena, CA: William Carey Library.

TWO

STEPS AND STUMBLES FORWARD

Truly, O God of Israel, our Savior, you work in mysterious ways.

~ Isaiah 45:15 (NLT)

The mysteriousness of God regularly reveals itself in some of the surprising ways that He chooses to accomplish His will. He used a boy with a slingshot to fight for Him (David), a murderer with a stutter to speak for Him (Moses), a virgin to bear His Son (Mary), and came as a helpless baby to establish His Kingdom (a surprise to everyone). It shouldn't then be surprising that in our lifetime He would choose another set of unconventional candidates—two post-college twenty-somethings—to spark a prayer movement that would last decades and contribute to rallying thousands of believers to active missional involvement spanning hemispheres.

It Only Takes A Spark

In the early part of 1990 Darren and Catherine, both in their mid-twenties and from the Cherry Hills Community Church (CHCC) college group, signed up for a short-term mission trip through a large mission agency. Their team was sent out and hosted by two long-term missionaries, James and Ayu, already at work among an unreached people group, the *Chantik*. The Chantik were a people known for being devout Muslims, practitioners of folk black magic, and zealous to maintain the right to practice both.

The trip was arduous, as all trips to locations a dozen or so time zones away are, with strange food and a sweaty climate. The whole experience was so far from the familiar that it was all but otherworldly. The Chantik had a duality about them, often friendly and curious, but also committed to dark practices that were inscrutable for a Western Christian to comprehend. "The spiritual darkness was palpable," recounted Catherine. Nevertheless, it was the glimmers of desire for hope that they saw in the Chantik people around them that sparked a fire in the two short-termers.

Catherine talked at length with James and Ayu about the Chantik. Her curiosity grew from details about the ministry being done to their future hopes. She probed James and Ayu about the need they might have for focused support from a church in America. With these questions asked and answered, Catherine and Darren came home with a unified vision to rally their church, Cherry Hills Community Church (CHCC), to adopt the Chantik.

Immediately upon their return, they approached Pastor G. and started the conversation rolling. Catherine shared her pictures, her stories, and her impressions of the need of the Chantik. Together they communicated the importance of the relationships they'd formed with James and Ayu as a gateway to an eternal opportunity to partner in what the Lord was doing in that part of the world. With Pastor G.'s ready help, the two twenty-somethings cast a vision of adoption for the church leadership and eventually the whole church. Their efforts resulted in rallying a megachurch in a Denver suburb to adopt an unreached people group thousands of miles away, proving that even a small rudder can change the path of a huge ship when divine pressure from the Holy Spirit is applied.

A Church Inspired

By the latter part of 1990, Cherry Hills formally adopted the Chantik with the vision *to plant an indigenous, self-supporting, reproducing church among the people.* It was a good goal, one that is still in some form in the process of being accomplished. However, because "adopting a people" was such a new thought at that time, there was no prescribed, surefire way of doing so. In those first couple of years, CHCC's pursuit of this adoption broke down into two main avenues: *to collaborate with those who know* and *to pray for and prep those who go.*

THOSE WHO KNOW

It was clear that this adoption was more ambitious than anything the church had tried before; they needed help from experts. Wisely, CHCC sought partnership with a missional agency known for its pioneering attitude and experience with unreached people groups in the eastern part of the world, one we'll call the *Venture Group.* They negotiated the expectations, one from another, about what partnering meant: how that would function in the development, training, sending, and supporting of a team of missionaries sent to the Chantik. This partnership was a critical step in the right direction to give the future long-term missionaries the logistical and spiritual support that they would need. This partnership was a critical beginning, but it wouldn't be enough on its own.

Cherry Hills knew they needed to involve even more people committed to the spread of the gospel among the Chantik. It would (and will) take the church acting in unity to make an impact in a land so engulfed in spiritual darkness. CHCC reached out to churches, individuals, mission organizations, and anyone interested in reaching the Chantik for Christ. It was then that the first of six "Chantik Consultations" was held—a forum regarding how to go, who was there, what had been tried, potential next steps, and, most of all, to pray for the Chantik.

The Holy Spirit was moving on behalf of the Chantik. As preparations for the consultation were under way, individuals, churches, and mission agencies across the country were sharing their interest in evangelizing the Chantik. The consultation brought those passionate believers together—all committed to see the Chantik come to know Christ—and that event helped catalyze the movement within Cherry Hills.

Pastors, staff, mission workers, seminarians, and hosts of lay people from Cherry Hills attended the consultation. The event laid the foundation of excitement within Cherry Hills so much that a group of believers subsequently banded together as the "Chantik Home Team," comprised of roughly forty laypeople. They were dedicated to energizing the church body and supporting staff efforts to inform others about the Chantik. Specifically, the Home Team's vision was to mobilize the members of Cherry Hills behind the adoption of the Chantik. That great and massive goal started with faithful prayer.

THOSE WHO GO

The Home Team, the outreach staff, and Pastor G. collectively were charged with motivating a then three-thousand-member church to learn about, pray for, and physically go to the Chantik—a people completely foreign to them and in a pre-Internet age. This formidable charge was faced with a similar degree of resolve as that which started the modern missions movement.

At a Baptist Missionary Society gathering in 1793, William Carey, father of the modern missions movement, said this to cofounder Andrew Fuller and the handful of pastors present:

> Our undertaking to India really appeared to me, on its commencement, to be somewhat like a few men, who were deliberating about the importance of penetrating into a deep mine, which had never before been explored, we had no one to guide us ..."
>
> And while [they] were thus deliberating, Carey, as it were, said, "Well, I will go down, if you will hold the rope."[1]

John Ryland, one of the pastors in attendance and the recorder of this exchange, said, "But before he went down . . . he, as it seemed to me, took an oath from each of us, at the mouth of the pit, to this effect— that 'while we lived, we should never let go of the rope.'"[2]

In the adoption of the Chantik, CHCC was also climbing down into the dark; but this band of believers at Cherry Hills, made up of staff and volunteers, took seriously the job of "holding the rope" for those who would eventually go to the Chantik. They knew it was their job to pave the way for the many—the whole church body—to get behind and involved in the adoption movement. That collective energy fueled momentum within the church for Pastor G. and the outreach staff to take the next big step forward: *to go to the Chantik.*

The First Of Many

The first of what has turned out to be twenty-four short-term team trips over twenty-five years was planned and taken in 1992. In that first trip, eight adults were sent out to the wilds of Chantikland; and, fortunately, James and Ayu—the long-term missionaries who were adopted along with the Chantik—acted as their guides. The team's first exposure to the people and their way of life was eye-opening.

Seeing where and how the Chantik lived was intriguing, but being exposed to what they had to deal with emotionally, spiritually, relationally, socially, and politically was especially shocking.

On one hand, the Chantik are a very family-oriented society, with numerous admirable qualities that make you want to be their friend. On the other hand, they were fighting a bloody civil war with the prevailing regional tribe in order to have the right to increase their adherence to Islam (among other issues). Specifically, they wanted the right to practice shari'a law—a religious legal system dictated by the Quran, which allows both corporal and capital punishment for anyone, Muslim or not, under the jurisdiction of the law.

The difficulties of evangelism didn't dampen the enthusiasm of adoption, but instead brought resolve to the members of that team and energy to the church.

Friendly and generous, yet strict and brutal, the Chantik world felt diametrically at odds to foreign onlookers who came with a "separation of church and state" mentality. When shari'a law is in effect, it supersedes national systems of law, and there is zero separation. The mosque is the law. That social, religious, and political climate creates (then and today) a palpable spiritual darkness that breeds an intense pressure to conform to Islamic beliefs and law. That pressure, with very real life-and-death implications, makes it painfully difficult for individuals in Chantikland to come to Christ.

The difficulties of evangelism didn't dampen the enthusiasm of adoption, but instead brought resolve to the members of that team and energy to the church. CHCC now had a taste of what the people were like, but they needed to know more. In this pre-Internet age,

Pastor G. initiated a relationship with a missions-focused research organization, The Project. Their focus was to help churches, agencies, and universities cultivate an understanding of unreached peoples by providing resources and leading in-country research trips. Cherry Hills hired The Project to do ethnographic research with an evangelistic perspective in order to provide in-depth information about the Chantik.

The underlying purpose of connecting with The Project, and commissioning the research, was to excite more than just eight to twelve people at a time with each short-term trip. The whole church needed to catch the vision. Cherry Hills needed to fan the sparks of enthusiasm into a full-blown fire of passionate commitment, putting the Chantik at the forefront of CHCC's prayers, hearts, and efforts. For that to happen, CHCC members needed to become familiar with those whose lives were so terribly distant from their own, both literally and figuratively.

Step one was to go. Step two was to go again, but with that purpose of gaining greater understanding as their motive. The Project, in collaboration with CHCC, sent a research team to make strategic firsthand observations and inquiries. They had to do it this way because no books on the Chantik were available, the Internet was a baby without its current breadth and depth, and the only way to get to know the Chantik was to go and be among them. The Project blended four CHCC church members into the six-person research team and spent three months living in Chantikland. They studied the people's lifestyle and rituals, and how their families and communities operated.

Upon returning home, the research team set out to articulate all they discovered, a process that took months, and yet the momentum in the church was ramping up in other ways. Pastor G. fielded countless questions from returning team members who were themselves contemplating full-time ministry among the Chantik. Between those conversations and connections made at the Chantik consultations, Pastor G. found himself in the initial stages of forming a team.

Messy Beginnings

The mid-90s saw a whirlwind of steps forward. But, as the saying goes, it was two steps forward and one step back. The church formalized the partnership with the mission agency—the Venture Group—and for several years the desire to go as part of the long-term team (the Go Team) was quite high for both individuals and couples. Seventeen people had "committed" to be part of the Go Team, and that didn't include the two partner-missionaries already in the field: James and Ayu.

Having that kind of enthusiasm and momentum was amazing, but dedicating their lives to the Lord like that inevitably makes people prime targets for the devil. With a total of nineteen people enthusiastic to claim Chantikland for the Lord, the enemy responded by trying to discourage, delay, and disassemble the vibrant group of would-be missionaries. Fortunately, we know that the Lord is an overcomer and no one throws us into the fire without Him managing the flames to refine the outcome. Despite any temporary victory of the devil, the Lord's ultimate purposes will be accomplished.

The Rally Cry

Simultaneously, while this fervor over joining the Go Team was reaching a fever pitch, The Project had formulated their research into a document that would rally the rest of the church to action. The Project, in cooperation with Pastor G. and the outreach department, published "A Prayer for the Chantik" (often called the "Chantik Prayer Guide")—a twenty-six-page booklet that broke down twelve major areas of information about the Chantik and provided seventy-two prayers to offer on their behalf. Pastor G.'s hope was to "rain down such a flood of prayer that it would start in the hill country of Chantikland and wash the evil out to sea, leaving in its wake the love of Christ."

This document was groundbreaking for the church. It provided faces, stories, details, and a sense of reality to these faraway people. It was the centerpiece of a major awareness campaign launched by the outreach department in celebration of the adoption of the Chantik. Awareness events were hosted. Fliers were distributed. Thousands of the prayer guides were distributed to the church body, raising the level of interest and concern well beyond the few who had traveled to Chantikland. Small groups across the church used the booklet as a guide to pray weekly for the Chantik. The church was fired up.

Logistical Nightmares

CHCC's ideal vision was to send out a team of diverse, but unified, members with a team leader who could rally the troops behind a solid strategy to accomplish the mission. That team would enter the province together and work in collaborative ways to accomplish the ultimate goal: *to plant an indigenous, self-supporting, reproducing church among the Chantik.*

Ideals are important to have; they encourage us to be paragons of virtue and to "shoot for the stars." The reality, however, is that life, with all of its complications, can be downright gut-wrenching at times. "But this I call to mind, and therefore I have hope: The steadfast love of the LORD never ceases, his mercies never come to an end," says the author of Lamentations.[3] And Paul, in a swell of encouragement, shares this poignant truth: "We know that all things work together for good to those who love God, to those who are the called according to *His* purpose."[4] God's love and goodness are the framework by which we can view less than ideal circumstances with an abiding sense of hope.

It is God's redemptive nature, along with His never-ending mercies, that allow us to view the roll out of the team as *all part of His ultimate plan.* By 1996, only ten of the seventeen individuals had gone through candidate school with the Venture Group to be a part of the Go Team. Several of the ten had raised their support and made it in-country the year before and were actively studying the language and getting a feel for the culture, while the rest of the team were still fund-raising and preparing for departure. And if you've ever talked to an aspiring missionary during the time they are trying to raise support, you know how frustrating the wait can be. Waiting isn't easy for any of us, but when you have a call from God burning a whole in your heart, waiting is torturous. Consequently, this was a challenging time to have the team split between different hemispheres. Specifically, having some Go Team members in-country as much as three years before the others turned out to be a caldron in which problems simmered.

The first of a series of problems was communication. What a reader today may not realize is that all of these events occurred before email had been popularized. Parts of Chantikland were extremely primitive, and accessing the Internet wasn't just difficult—it simply didn't exist. And even phones rarely worked for the first several years. When you could get the phones to work, the time difference made for challenges. And mailing something took ages, if it arrived at all. The logistics of getting the various team members in the field, and hearing updates from the field, were collectively brutal. Add to the poor and stilted communication the fact that the team leaders, Tim and Sandy, were the very last to join the team in the field (their story is told in chapter 6) and you can see that challenges to unity would be a central problem in the next few years of the journey.

Go Team members went in-country from as early as January 1995 to as late as March 1998. To stem the tide of disconnectedness, the church hosted periodic team gatherings with the intent to build relationships, trust, shared vision, and a team mentality among the disparate members of the Chantik Go Team. Those goals proved nearly impossible. In light of the hampered communication, the distance, and the lack of a unified vision, it's no surprise that personality conflicts arose. *Isn't it fortunate, then, that we serve a redemptive God through whom all things are possible?*[5]

What Is A Team?

By the spring of 1998, Cherry Hills finally had the semblance of a team in place in-country. From the original seventeen who joined the Go Team, only six members—two couples and two individuals—made it in-country. Within six months of the team being together, only four of those members would move from the city where the language school was to finally enter the province of the Chantik as the Cherry Hills Chantik Go Team. Details of this team's work will be shared in subsequent chapters, but remember: "Your enemy the devil prowls around like a roaring lion looking for someone to devour."[6] The enemy wasn't just going to let these brave missionaries come into the land without a fight. The devil lashed out in the form of team conflict and illness; and by the end of 1999, only two of the four team members were left on the Cherry Hills Go Team who were still in the region working among the Chantik.

You might be tempted to be discouraged at this point in the story, but don't forget that God is in control and that He has a redemptive vision for all His servants to accomplish His purposes in the world.

Of the original seventeen who wanted to be a part of the Go Team, fifteen remained devoted to the region through their various efforts both in-country and stateside. Specifically, eight members went to be long-term missionaries with various teams—including the CHCC Go Team—and the other seven went on repeated short-term trips and were involved in all manner of endeavors at home to support the work among the Chantik.

Take Beth, for example. She went through the candidate school and was an official Go Team member, but she felt called to be a home-based member. She worked stateside as the team advocate in the church and contributed vitally to communication between the team in the field and the church staff and body. In those pre-email/Internet days, her contribution was crucial.

So while the original vision was a clean A→B plan, where CHCC would send a team to plant churches, the Lord—whether by design or through His redemptive nature—instead had more of a "pool table split" endgame in mind. Obviously, having all the players go in different directions wasn't the original plan; but God, in His redemptive wisdom, eventually got each one to a place where He could use them. That is the best outcome.

The Amazing Thing About Prayer

While all the team formation and launching was happening, it was through the Chantik Prayer Guide, generated by the research team, that the church body learned to pray in a focused way about the needs of the people—their spiritual, relational, physical, and emotional needs. Specifically, the twelve sections of the guide, which functioned like weekly devotionals, each had six prayers—collectively numbering seventy-two prayers. The strategy was that all the small groups across the church would be learning about, and praying for, the Chantik in a powerful way *at the same time.* Talk about focused prayer!

Our Lord, who hears the cries of His faithful servants, heard the thousands of Cherry Hills Community Church members who prayed tens of thousands of prayers for the Chantik. And though numerous strongholds remain fiercely in place, and the battle for Chantikland is still being waged, Satan should be worried. Those spiritual walls *will* come tumbling down.

The Bottom Line

Evaluating the adoption of the Chantik twenty-five years later, we can see that through all the strife and toil *the Lord has answered dozens of those initial seventy-two prayers*—whether in part, in full, or for a time. The next handful of chapters share the stories of eight long-term missionaries, working among the Chantik, who collectively have given 150 years of service in the field.

Though Paul said it first in 2 Corinthians 1:8-11, the essence of these verses could have been a letter home from any of our missionaries:

> We do not want you to be uninformed, brothers and sisters, about the troubles we experienced in the province of Asia. We were under great pressure, far beyond our ability to endure, so that we despaired of life itself. Indeed, we felt we had received the sentence of death. But this happened that we might not rely on ourselves but on God, who raises the dead. He has delivered us from such a deadly peril, and He will deliver us again. On Him we have set our hope that He will

continue to deliver us, as you help us by your prayers. Then many will give thanks on our behalf for the gracious favor granted us *in answer to the prayers of many.*[7]

Just like Paul didn't want the Corinthians to be uninformed, neither should you be uninformed about both the strife and the victories experienced by these missionaries. We, as believers, need to trust that the Lord is working all things together for good, and simultaneously be like Abraham begging for any righteous among the people to be spared.[8] We need to turn our prayers to the Lord, like the persistent widow,[9] and plead for the Chantik, and all the lost children of the world, to have ears to hear the saving message of Christ's love.

In the meanwhile, let us revel together in how the Lord has answered the prayers of many through stories from Chantikland.

Chapter 2 Citations

1. Joseph Ivimey, *A History of the English Baptists.* London: printed for the author, and sold by Burditt, Button, Hamilton, Baynes, 1811.
2. Ibid.
3. Holy Bible. Revised Standard Version. Lamentations 3:21-22.
4. Holy Bible. New King James Version. Romans 8:28.
5. Holy Bible. New King James Version. Matthew 19:26.
6. Holy Bible. New International Version. 1 Peter 5:8b.
7. Holy Bible. New International Version. 2 Corinthians 1:8-11.
8. Holy Bible. New International Version. Genesis 18:16-33.
9. Holy Bible. New King James Version. Luke 18:1-8.

THREE

James, Ayu, and the Long Haul

All the world's a stage,
And all the men and women merely players;
They have their exits and their entrances,
And one man in his time plays many parts.

~William Shakespeare, *As You Like It*

Shakespeare had it right when he penned that we are all players on the grand stage of life and are privileged to play many roles. What he failed to consider, in this passage at least, is the playwright in his scenario—God Almighty. For it is this playwright who orchestrates the casting of each role, the timing of entrances and exits, and where in His great play of history a scene unfolds. We, as the players, determine *how* to perform; but it is the Lord, in His sovereignty, who lays the stage and gives us the opportunities to do His will. Paul, in Ephesians 2:10, explains: "We are God's handiwork, created in Christ Jesus to do good works, which God prepared in advance for us to do."[1]

With that thought of advanced preparation in mind, it is likewise easy to consider that if God has prepared good works for us to do, He may also have to get us to the right place physically, mentally, emotionally, relationally, and spiritually so that we would then be prepared for that work. Therefore, to get us to "that" place, He may need us to move upstage or downstage—or to a stage in another part of the world—for us to be ready for *our scene*.

Ayu's Path – A Story That Actually Happened

Ayu's family had settled among a tribe not their own, one that lived in a rural region of their home country. Both her grandparents and parents were assigned to the region through their jobs, and options to leave were quite limited and often unrealistic. So, they endured. They lived as persecuted minorities in a volatile region. And whether the Lord orchestrated this time, or simply redeemed it, this familial history would be a critical piece in setting the course of Ayu's future. Her family was, after all, among the very few Christians living in a highly Muslim community, in a highly Muslim region—*Chantikland*.

Shortly after college, Ayu felt the Lord calling her to something other than the traditional job she had taken. Through long hours of prayer, she made the decision to leave a good job and join the organization that two of her younger sisters were missionaries with— which we'll call *Resolve*. But instead of training in the country of her birth, as they had, she felt the Lord calling her to train in Singapore of all places!

Knowing absolutely nothing about Singapore, she bought a book about the small island nation. It was only then that she realized English was the major language spoken there, a language in which she knew how to say exactly three things: "Coca-Cola," "photocopy," and "hello." In her mind, this was a devastating blow to where she felt the Lord was leading her.

Out of desperation and frustrated irritation, she challenged the Lord. She asked God for three seemingly impossible things:

1. The money for the training school fees.
2. A round-trip ticket to Singapore.
3. The language, English.

Ayu, who was young and immature in her faith at this point, had the same kind of "I dare You" conversation with the Lord that many of us have had. What follows, however, is the Lord responding rather like He did to Job when He thundered, "Where were you when I laid the foundations of the earth? Tell me, if you know so much."[2] Without question, the Lord was about to show Ayu just how big He *was, is,* and *always will be.*

Later that day, still confused and disheartened, Ayu turned to her mother. She needed encouragement from this strong Christian woman who labored endlessly for her children in prayer. Together they discussed the matter and prayed, but chose to keep the conversation and the details of Ayu's prayer to themselves.

The day following her prayer, a family friend approached Ayu to talk. At that moment Ayu was engrossed in a conversation with friends, so she hesitated to leave to talk to the man. Noticing the pause, he handed her an envelope, said goodbye, and walked away. Not thinking much of it, Ayu put the envelope in her purse and continued her lunch.

A short time later, at home in the kitchen with her mother, she remembered the envelope and opened it. From it she withdrew a *round-trip ticket to Singapore,* good for one year, which had her name on it. The family friend had no way of knowing about her prayer, and more unbelievable still was that the Lord had just used a devout Muslim to jump one of her seemingly *impossible* hurdles. Still reeling from the shock of the ticket, Ayu and her mother were surprised by her father's early return home. He never left work early, and yet, there he was in the kitchen just after lunch handing her a second envelope, saying, "Here, I think this is for you."

As it turned out, an associate of Ayu's father had closed a very big deal, and upon returning to the office he handed Ayu's father an envelope and said, "I think one of your daughters needs this." Though not knowing what was in the envelope, and not being a Christian at the time either, her father had a gut feeling. Out of all of his thirteen children, including five daughters, this envelope was for Ayu—and he needed to give it to her right away.

Upon opening the second envelope, Ayu found $1,500 inside, which was enough money to cover her school fees with some left over. This businessman, like the first, was a devoted Muslim. No one but Ayu's mother had any idea about what she was feeling called to, or the details of her prayer, and yet the Lord had used all three of these men to answer the first two aspects of her prayer.

Upon opening the second envelope, Ayu found $1,500.00 cash inside, which was enough money to cover her school fees with some left over.

Overwhelmed by the Lord's hand in answering her prayer, Ayu felt a sense of urgency to go to the training as soon as possible. In a week's time she had gotten her passport (a complete miracle in itself) and flown to Singapore to join the next training session, which started that week. It wasn't until she was walking off the plane and was greeted by her welcoming committee that she remembered one crucial detail: *she still didn't know English*. In a panic, Ayu just smiled and nodded in hopes that they wouldn't notice she had no idea what they were saying. Within minutes it was clear to everyone that she didn't speak English, not even a little.

Deeply embarrassed by not knowing English, Ayu would take long walks to try to avoid her classmates instead of engaging with them. One girl, however, a roommate in the dorm, did speak a dialect similar to one of Ayu's languages. Between classes Ayu would ask as many questions as she could of the girl, but for two grueling weeks she sat through class after class absorbing nothing.

Waves of confusion and failure swept over her one night until she cried out to God in a way she never had before. Through wrenching sobs she acknowledged that the language had become a wall between her and the Lord. She repented of her "I'll figure it out myself" attitude, which characterized the first two weeks of classes. And in utter exhaustion, Ayu fell asleep accepting that the next day she would go home.

The next morning, Ayu joined the girls from her dorm room in the cafeteria and asked them to forgive her for crying so loudly in the night. She shared that the Lord had really met her in prayer and that she felt much better now. In astonished silence, her classmates listened to Ayu apologize—*in English*. No one said a thing. *Because, really, what do you say after you witness a miracle?* Instead, they all bustled off to chapel, and it was only then that Ayu realized she understood the English she was hearing. Ayu could read, write, and speak English fluently! In the night, the Lord had blessed her miraculously with the language—the final *impossible* hurdle.

What Ayu saw as impossible simply turned into three more miracles we can attribute to God's greatness. He had a plan for her life; and *being sent to Singapore, receiving the gift of English overnight,* and *being raised in Chantikland* were the foundation of that plan.

The Journey Of James

It was in Singapore that James's life intersected with Ayu's, but that is far from where his story started. Born in the Midwest, James grew up in the suburbs of a large city and attended a nondenominational

Protestant church. The church of his youth was not only where he found Christ, but that congregation supports his ministry to this day.

In seventh grade James accepted Christ as his Savior, but it wasn't until he had graduated high school and trade school that he started thinking seriously about his future and how he could serve the Lord. During a baseball game sponsored by the church, James found himself deep in conversation with an acquaintance. This man had gone to a three-month training school for believers run by none other than the missionary organization Resolve. He strongly suggested James attend the school and then participate in the placement afterward, in which students minister somewhere in the world for an additional three months.

This was it. This was the great idea James had been looking for to jump-start his future. In a blink, he had joined Resolve, completed training, and begun actively ministering in a long-term capacity throughout the Eastern Hemisphere.

While on staff with Resolve, his first couple of years were spent in various Asian locations, learning and growing in his faith and capacity as a missionary. As time went on, he accepted an opportunity to lead an outreach team, which required relocation to the Singapore headquarters of Resolve.

After packing for his relocation all day in the blistering heat, late one Thursday evening James boarded his flight to Singapore. Given the late hour of his flight and the miserable conditions while packing, it didn't bother him at all that he was showing up in a tattered T-shirt, shorts, and flip-flops. He assumed he'd just be shown to his living quarters and he could meet the team refreshed after a good night's sleep.

When James stepped off the plane, he was greeted by a man who spoke only a little English. Since they couldn't really communicate, James sat back and let the man drive him to the Resolve headquarters in near silence. He quickly learned that the Resolve base took up the top three floors of a skyscraper in downtown Singapore.

What James didn't realize as he traveled up to the fifteenth floor was that this particular HQ had an open-house style worship event every Thursday night in which all the staff were required to dress in their Sunday best to greet newcomers, and as a very well attended event, it ran quite

> Disheveled and tired, James watched the elevator doors open to a sea of well-dressed churchgoers.

late. Disheveled and tired, James watched the elevator doors open to a sea of well-dressed churchgoers. Near the elevator, a girl with dark hair and a pretty smile looked at James. She said just a few words, in a foreign language, to his companion. The man briefly answered, and with that the elevator doors closed and the two men started their journey back to the lobby. With one glance and a few words, James had been *kicked out.*

"And who was this girl who kicked him out?" you might be asking. That's right, it was *Ayu.* The woman, who would become his wife less than two years later, kicked him out upon first sight. Clearly, James makes a much better second impression!

Together, They Were Called

James and Ayu ministered well together in Singapore, and initially, they had no plans to leave. However, James's work with the unreached people group focused team (UPG-focused team) led him and Ayu to take an exploratory trip throughout Asia to visit a half-dozen of the hardest-to-reach people groups.

In the spring of 1989, at the end of several months of traveling, they arrived finally in Ayu's homeland, which itself held several of the hardest-to-reach peoples, including the Chantik. They had arrived four or five days before their final flight home to Singapore, and Ayu knew how close they were to the southern border of Chantikland. She suggested they go see her childhood home with their remaining time and James readily agreed.

They made their first trip together into Chantikland. They visited her home, the compound where her father worked, and the surrounding village. Then, Ayu asked if they could drive a little further to visit her brother's grave. He had died in a tragic motorcycle accident when she was in middle school, and it had been many years since the family had lived near enough to visit the grave.

The next morning, they rose early and went to the graveyard. Early morning light played off the mist and shadows surrounding her brother's grave, as they sat and reveled in the powerful sense of the Lord's presence. His glory seemed to fill the air, and Ayu began to weep. Visiting Chantikland had taken its toll, bringing back many painful memories from her childhood—the loss of her brother, the persecution, and the turbulence within her family as a result of those factors and more. She and James cried, prayed, and listened to the Lord.

And like the old hymn says, "Up from the grave He arose" . . . with a mighty vision in their hearts. James and Ayu both had a clear sense that the Lord was calling them to make Chantikland their home, their ministry, and His harvest. He, the God of the universe, Savior of the world, and Conqueror over death, was calling them to bring the Good News of the gospel and freedom in Christ to the Chantik, whom they sensed were oppressed with a great weight of death and hopelessness.

It wasn't until James and Ayu returned to Singapore and looked at a calendar that they realized the morning they had spent in the graveyard was actually the morning of Easter Sunday. They had traveled for so long that they had lost track of the days, but the Lord hadn't. He chose the celebration of Christ's resurrecting power over death as the day He would call them to work among the Chantik, a calling that was decades in the making.

The resonating Easter imagery of Christ as the Conqueror over death, the bringer of freedom, the Redeemer of the lost, the one who can bring life in the midst of death—*that* is the hope we have for all the unreached peoples of the world. And, consequently, that is how the Lord brought two workers, from faraway places in the world, to sow seeds and to reap on behalf of the Kingdom the great harvest that He can see in Chantikland.

• • •

The following stories illustrate answers to prayers in part, in full, or for a time. Specifically, answers to those prayers from the Chantik Prayer Guide published in the early 1990s with the help of an organization called The Project. Originally, the guide was designed as a publication simply to inform CHCC about their adopted people, but it also included seventy-two prayers for small groups and individuals to pray through in their weekly study.

THE FIRST DOMINO

PRAYER #19 (from the Chantik Prayer Guide): *"Ask the Lord of the harvest to send laborers to the Chantik—that they may know Jesus and then influence many ethnic groups."*

James and Ayu moved to Chantikland in the spring of 1990. This strategic placement of two remarkable Kingdom ambassadors would turn out to be one of the Lord's key moves in accomplishing the endgame of an established Christ-worshiping church among the Chantik. He christened their faithfulness in relocating by sending the first of many short-term teams just a month or so after their arrival in the region. This team, organized through a mission agency, included Darren and Catherine from Cherry Hills Community Church.

Well-seasoned as missionaries, and acutely knowledgeable of the Chantik, James and Ayu were positioned perfectly as the first true partners for CHCC in the work among the Chantik. This partnership endures today, and a large aspect of their ministry for the last quarter of a century has been in hosting and launching short-term teams and sending teams of church planters into Chantikland.

Short-term teams (from Cherry Hills and several dozen other churches and organizations that partner with James and Ayu) have come in such great numbers over the years that James and Ayu have lost count of how many teams they've hosted. The numbers aren't just in the dozens, but rather dozens upon dozens and even scores upon scores, of teams who've had this faithful couple act as their guides. And, they've done it for over twenty-five years.

Teams from around the world—from Colorado and New Zealand, Southern California and the Philippines, Florida, Germany, and Austria, and from across Asia—have connected with James and Ayu to reach the Chantik. The multiplication factor of their impact was, and is, immense.

Collectively, the many hundreds of people who comprise those teams have sown seeds of salvation as they've ministered through their example, words, and prayer for decades now. While we know from the parable of the sower (Luke 8) that not all seeds land on fertile ground, that knowledge should divinely inspire believers around the world as they pray for the lost. Pray that every seed of truth sown would be protected from the choking weeds of non-Christ-centered culture (be it in the media or from the worship of a false god). Pray that the vultures of the devil won't snatch away potential rebirth in a person who has heard the truth. Finally, pray that brave long-term and short-term missionaries continue to water and feed the seeds sown, so that no burgeoning believer withers in isolation.

A SEASON FOR EVERYTHING

PRAYER #49: *"Pray that God would raise up Christians who desire to share the gospel of Jesus while teaching English to avid Chantik learners."*

The Lord has answered this particular prayer, time and again, in different seasons of the work among the Chantik. However, the first iteration of openness to help from the West came with the brainchild of an important collaboration. James and Ayu made the acquaintance of a man we'll call Andrew in 1989; this connection then opened the doors to countless future missionaries entering Chantikland.

A gifted innovator, Andrew's job as a staff member of the Southern Baptist mission agency was to think of new ways to get people into hard-to-get places. James and Ayu were well-placed both on their UPG-team through Resolve and in the field in Chantikland among one of the hardest-to-reach people. Together, they were the perfect team to pioneer new avenues for ministry.

They identified a genuine need in Chantikland and cleverly thought to fulfill it in such a way that would bless the Chantik *and* allow them to receive visas for entry into the country. The need for the Chantik (all of the Chantik, not just the wealthy who lived in the cities) was to learn English. The answer was simple: import missionaries as English teachers. Though this is now a common practice in the mission world, it was still cutting-edge thinking at the time!

Together, James, Ayu, and Andrew worked to start an education organization that we'll call English Around the World (EAW). James handled all the legal paperwork in-country and Andrew did the work out of the country. Before they knew it, both men were up to their ears recruiting missionaries to be English teachers because the program was found to be highly desirable by the Chantik government. In an uncharacteristic show of favor, the EAW was granted visas hand over fist, totaling thirty to forty visas in its heyday!

The program was specifically designed to teach high school English teachers *better* English through regular opportunities to converse with native-English speakers. On an eternal level, this was an unbelievable opportunity to share the love of Christ relationally. The virtue of regular conversation is that all the normal niceties will soon wear thin, and eventually, as a bond grows, the Chantik teacher may feel free to ask questions of the "foreigner"—of whom they must be quite curious. Then the door was opened for the missionary to answer all manner of questions and evangelize as the opportunities availed themselves.

On a temporal level of providing practical help, it was well known in Chantikland that those who could speak English could obtain better-paying jobs, ones typically out of reach for the poor in wealth and education. By teaching the teachers better, that benefit would trickle down to all their many students, who would then have a better foundation in the language. This program made ministry in all parts of the population achievable, whether in remote villages or the capital city, because the schools in which they were assigned to teach spanned the entire region.

Favor on the EAW program led to the doors swinging wide open for missionaries to enter the highly restrictive region of Chantikland. In fact, the EAW would later sponsor visas for several of our CHCC Go Team missionaries. The EAW likely would have continued to flourish, but the civil war in Chantikland gained intensity. It got to the point where English teachers were evacuated, and the government just stopped issuing the visas. The program may not have lasted forever, but those six years certainly represented a blessed season of openness to help from the West.

AN ANGEL ON THE ROAD

PRAYER #29: *"Pray for imams, and other community leaders to . . . [put] the good of their people above their own good."*

PRAYER #61: *"Pray for the devil's schemes to be thwarted so that the minds of the Chantik Muslims will see "the light of the gospel that displays the glory of Christ, who is the image of God."*

Ayu, James, and a number of others (recounted in later chapters of this book) had an extraordinary opportunity to be image-bearers of God Almighty to the helpless of the Chantik during an intense season of the civil war. They were bringers of hope and provision in the midst of chaos and despair. Generally, wars defy simple explanations. The very simple explanation of this civil war, however, was that the rebels wanted Chantikland to secede from their home nation, thereby becoming their own nation in control of their finances, resources, and religious rights. But the national army wasn't going to let that happen. As a result, the war ebbed and raged for some thirty years.

Chantikland was divided—the rebels lived mostly in the mountain villages and the national army occupied the cities. The success of the EAW program meant that their English teachers were stationed throughout districts across Chantikland, in the mountains *and* the cities. Years into the EAW teaching program, the fighting began to worsen. EAW workers were pulled from the field for their safety, because war was erupting on the streets and the normal routine of life and schooling had evaporated, especially in the mountain districts. The war was sporadic, popping up here one month only to pop up somewhere else the next. However, as teachers came into the capital city on their way out of the region, they informed James and Ayu of a dangerous trend. All the villagers would hide in the mosques in an attempt to flee from the fighting. It was a relatively good plan, if the fighting was short-term. Unfortunately, the violence was so severe between the rebels and the national army that the villagers were too afraid to come out of the mosques. Some of the battles would last weeks on end, so the villagers holed up in the mosques were beginning to starve.

The people needed food. Ayu and James had several businesses, one of which was raising chickens. The answer seemed clear. Unfortunately, the army wasn't allowing Westerners out of the city and the starving villagers were up in the hills. In light of the restrictions, James and the rest of the Cherry Hills Go Team couldn't leave the city—rendering delivery of the food up to the bold and courageous five-foot-nothing tall native of Chantikland, Ayu.

They slaughtered hundreds of chickens and packed them into their white van along with sugar, rice, flour, cooking oil, and more. Ayu took a couple of her local employees with her and drove up and down deserted roads with evidence of the war littering the way. Mosque after mosque, she would approach the building with food in hand and say, "You may not want it, but this food is given to you in the name of Jesus."

To this day, Ayu still remembers their answer: "We will accept this food from Jesus because we have nothing." As she returned again and again with food and medical supplies, her white van became known as "the angel," because she and her workers were the only ones on the road bringing help to the refugees in the mosques.

Thank God the imams allowed the acceptance of the food, because they could have refused. They could have let the people starve as a means of asserting their authority, but they didn't. Prayer #29, regarding imams and community leaders: answered!

Furthermore, the Lord wanted to reveal more glory in this situation. Instead of letting the devil have any victory from the masses huddling in mosques to survive, the Lord thwarted Satan's scheme to claim more lives—He provided food, in the name of the one and only Savior. Christ was proclaimed again and again as the provider of that temporal salvation from starvation; and in the act, we can only

1000s
OF CIVIL WAR
REFUGEES
FED

hope that the Holy Spirit was working, then and now, to communicate to those Muslim refugees that Jesus Christ is more than a momentary savior—He is *the* Savior. He is the bread of life eternal (John 6:35). Prayer #61, regarding the devil's schemes: answered!

It is critical to keep the *long view* in mind when it comes to missionary work. Our mighty Lord absolutely can work in singular moments to radically bring people to know Him (e.g., Saul/Paul on the Damascus road). But more often than not, He works out His plan of redemption in decades, centuries, and millennia. The lengths to which God, and His servants, will go to show the glory of Christ as a light in this dark world is evidence of His great love for the lost.

THE DAY AFTER

PRAYER #50: *"Pray that God would raise up Christians with skills in community development work (computer education, agriculture, sanitation, health, dental, and urban planning) to serve the Chantik people tangibly as well as eternally."*

In recent years, the world has been shown in excruciating detail natural disaster after natural disaster as the frequency and violence of each event gains more media coverage. Hurricane Katrina. The earthquake in Haiti. The earthquakes/tsunamis in Japan. The hurricane that hit the Philippines. The Indian Ocean earthquake and tsunami. Superstorm Sandy. The earthquake in Sichuan Province, China. The floods in the United Kingdom. The earthquakes/tsunamis in Chile.

The media shows the wreckage, but because of sensitivity to viewers, they can never show the most horrible part. The bodies. The hellish heaps of bodies that once were vibrant lives being lived. One of these unbelievably horrific events hit Chantikland some years ago.

Early one morning, on a day that dawned bright with the possibilities of family time and relaxation, a natural disaster hit Chantikland with such terrifying force that roughly 250,000 people were wiped out in less than ten minutes. In just moments, roughly five percent of the population died. Survivors and victims ran in every direction seeking refuge that for many would not come. The instant chaos spread terror.

It is hard to conceive of the kind of destruction that can be caused to life, to infrastructure, and to the hopes of those who live beyond a natural disaster of this caliber. Enduring the loss of family members is hard enough, but to deal with the ambiguity of just not knowing what happened to them is excruciating. Beyond that, the repetitive horror of waking up each morning to witness the wreckage of your world collectively created an unparalleled sense of hopelessness in Chantikland, a living hell.

At the time of the disaster, James and Ayu were not living in Chantikland, but just outside of it. However, their ministry was still centered in evangelism and outreach to the Chantik. They owned and ran businesses in the capital city of Chantikland, and they were actively sending teams on a regular basis. All of this required traveling into the region regularly, so they kept their former home in the capital city as a base camp for the significant time they spent there each month.

When the disaster hit, their fifteen team members were in its path; and for the first twenty-four hours after the event, the fate of the team was unclear. James and Ayu called everyone they could think of, both friends and officials. Everyone who would normally be in charge of dealing with disasters—government officials, police and firemen, even the army—they were all unreachable.

Though details were sparse and hard to get for the first twenty-four hours after the event, the magnitude of the loss of life and amount of damage was clearly staggering. The national military flew helicopters in to assess the regional airport. They radioed back that while no other facilities of the airport had survived (i.e., the tower had toppled and buildings had tumbled), the strip appeared to be serviceable.

While attempting to figure out his next move, James received a call from a pastor friend who lived a two-hour flight away. Hearing of the devastation in Chantikland, the pastor told James that he had a group of doctors and nurses jumping on a chartered plane and headed his way. The pastor wanted James to lead the team of medical people, and the three tons of medical supplies they put together, into Chantikland. It made sense. James knew the roads, the people, the language, and how to get things done. And, he needed a ride.

Only a handful of hours after that phone call, and roughly twenty-four hours after the disaster, James boarded the plane with the medical team of ten doctors and nurses, a logistics guy, and the pilots. They flew into the Chantikland regional airport hoping to land. Upon arrival, they opened the doors to witness complete chaos.

Thousands of people swarmed the airport beyond the landing strip in hopes to flee the disaster. Through the throngs they spotted two military trucks driving slowly out of the airport. With quick thinking, James sprinted into action and ran after the trucks. He waved them down and learned that these two trucks were potentially all that was left of the military. The army base was in the capital city, which was wholly devastated, and these soldiers had been spared simply because they had been on a delivery run when the disaster occurred. The soldiers were now cut off from their command and uncertain about their next move.

Determined to find his team and get these doctors to where they could do some good, James convinced the soldiers to transport himself, the medical personnel, and the three tons of supplies into the city. While the soldiers were willing, the effort was arduous. All the major roads were mangled with debris that made the roads all but impassable. The trucks labored over the broken infrastructure and wreckage. Progress forward often required clearing roads by hand and sometimes making new ones to successfully make it into the capital.

James directed the caravan to the first of four locations where his team could be: the shop house. He thought it would be a good location for the doctors to work out of; and if his team wasn't there, he would go on looking at the other locations.

Upon driving up, James saw the door to the shop standing open. Before he could jump from the truck, he saw his longtime friend Dek, a Chantik man, emerge from the shop with a mattress on his head. Seeing James, Dek screamed, dropped the mattress, and ran to the truck. "James! James! James!" Dek shouted, as he embraced James in a bear hug.

And just then, Donnie (James's team leader) walked out of the shop with a mattress flopping over his face. He heard Dek's shouts and said, "This is no time to joke. Come on, let's get out of here."

James called out to Donnie, and when Donnie realized that James was actually there, he ran into James's embrace. Both Donnie and Dek were filthy, barely clothed, and still reeling from the shock of the disaster—and now the shock of seeing James.

While still embracing Donnie, James asked, "Is your wife OK?" Donnie nodded yes.

"Are your kids OK?" More nodding.

"Is the team OK?" And with big sighs and nods Donnie affirmed that everyone on the team had survived.

Donnie pulled back, looked James intensely in the eye, and said, "I cannot believe you came for me!"

"I not only came for you," James replied, "but I brought ten doctors, three tons of medical supplies, and the military to look for you, your family, and the team." At this, the grief of the disaster and the relief of rescue comingled to create hysterical, yet justifiable, crying and hugging from both Donnie and Dek.

After a long time of consoling the men, James looked around at the unconscionable devastation that filled every inch of view. James had found his team, and it was time to help the survivors wandering the streets looking for their family members among the dead and wounded. Many of them didn't even realize how shell-shocked they were from the trauma of the disaster.

They relocated to a safer building, with less damage, and the medical team got straight to work setting up a clinic and helping those who could be saved. Donnie brought the men of the team to help the doctors set up, while the women cared for the children and cooked what little food they could find. Less than two days after the disaster, they had a clinic up and running and caring for the droves of suffering survivors.

PART 2: THE LONG DAYS AFTER

Continued answering of PRAYER #50: *"Pray that God would raise up Christians with skills in community development work (computer education, agriculture, sanitation, health, dental, and urban planning) to serve the Chantik people tangibly as well as eternally."*

The need for critical medical attention was relatively short and within a span of weeks all efforts turned to the massive cleanup effort (of the bodies and debris) and then on to the long-term projects of recovery: sanitation, community development, and education. The world was eager to help in the aftermath of the disaster, and within days of the event, NGOs (nongovernmental organizations) started showing up in droves. Millions of dollars had already been raised by these organizations, and more donations would come.

At first, anyone from anywhere was welcome to help in whatever way they could, but after about six months the Chantik government demanded NGOs to partner with local nonprofit organizations, and specifically only those that were present in Chantikland prior to the disaster. Governmental officials threatened to make this a law. Organizations like the Red Cross, Samaritan's Purse, Doctors Without Borders, World Vision, the United Nations, Habitat for Humanity, and Catholic Relief Services were being told that if they wanted to help, they needed to find local partners to do so.

With millions of dollars at their disposal, NGOs who needed to partner with established local nonprofits had their prayers answered before they even asked.[3] James and Ayu had started a nonprofit community development and education organization a decade before the disaster, and it came in handy for just such a time as this. All the organizations just mentioned, and more, coordinated their resources—money and personnel—through James and Ayu's nonprofit organization. While the government never did pass a law, its threats ended up driving funds and resources through these Kingdom workers who knew and loved the Chantik deeply.

In the first six weeks alone, over forty-nine thousand people received free medical attention through their clinics and the mobile clinics that traveled around in vans. In the eighteen months following the disaster, the Chantik government held the doors wide open to international aid agencies, including those that were faith-based. In that time, and through James and Ayu's organization, the NGOs were able to create programs to impact and benefit every aspect of social welfare for the survivors of the disaster.

Programs to distribute food were put into place, because entire crops had been ruined and some of the fields in which healthy crops once grew would require years to recover. Orphans were housed and cared for and sports programs were implemented to bring back some levity to the emotionally devastated youth. English and computer classes gave opportunities to the poor by providing skills that command a higher wage. Medical relief. Vocational training. Microfinance lending. Agriculture projects. Building homes and schools. Training teachers. And new businesses, lots of new businesses, were started by the people and for the people of Chantikland.

OPPORTUNITY COMES CALLING

PRAYER #57: *"Pray for openings for poor Chantik people to gain good employment, even if they have no rich connections."*

"Who you know" shouldn't be the determining factor in a person's success. But let's be realistic, it matters in the West just like it does in Chantikland. The system in that region caters to the rich getting all the choice positions in the working world, thereby leading to further prosperity for the few. Whereas the poor—well, they are left to their own devices with little to no hope of betterment. The natural disaster turned everything like that in Chantikland upside down.

The capital city was one of the hardest hit areas in the disaster. With one terrible blow, roughly 40 percent of the workforce was gone. Functionally, that created thousands of job openings and business opportunities aplenty to meet all the new demands of recovery. Possibly for the first time in Chantik history, both *opportunity* and *training and education* (through NGOs) were available to the poor. People who never would have had a chance previously were now finding opportunities in business. This was particularly the case because many businesses were started for the exact purpose of helping survivors generate a new life after the tragedy.

Not all of the jobs survived after the NGOs eventually pulled out. Many of the opportunities, in fact, faded away. But for a time, they were like air to a drowning people.

· · ·

The beauty of bringing business into the ministry equation in a place like Chantikland is that it helps in the short-term by providing stability for families, self-respect for the worker, and energy to the local economy. In the long-term, opportunities for life-on-life relational evangelism between the workers, owners, and the missionaries are abundant. In these hard-to-reach places of the world, it is the spiritual darkness, not just the physical terrain, that makes people hard to reach. When the devil has strongholds in a place for decades—or worse, for centuries, as is the case with Chantikland—shortsighted efforts at evangelizing aren't effective in bringing people to Christ.

Successful evangelism among the unreached people of the world typically looks like year after year of believers living as examples of how different a life with Christ can be. These missionaries are ambassadors for Christ,[4] showing nonbelievers that they are trustworthy—and the One they serve is as well. *That* is what makes lasting headway for the gospel, and that is the kind of ministry the apostle Peter meant when he said, "Always be prepared to give an answer to everyone who asks you to give the reason for the hope that you have. But do this with gentleness and respect."[5]

Peter knew that light in the darkness can't help but stand out. People will notice. Those in the dark will wonder and marvel at the light, and as the Holy Spirit woos them to Himself, they will muster the courage to ask questions.

Peter said to be ready when they ask but to answer with gentleness and respect, because he knew that they would be skittish and fearful as they reach into the light, especially for the first time. In the light, every sin and sinner is exposed; it is a very vulnerable place to be. Therefore, we as believers must be gentle with those coming to grips with their desperate need for a Savior, knowing that we too had to step into the light.

IN THE NAME OF JESUS

PRAYER #12: *"Pray that the Chantik people would know the truth, and that the truth would set them free."*

In a "two birds with one stone" stroke of genius, James and Ayu started businesses almost as soon as they moved to Chantikland—some for profit, some not-for-profit. These businesses established their legitimacy in the region to the local authorities (even when the civil war reached a fever pitch), and it provided consistent access to long-term visas for James as an employee of the company. When most Americans were being expelled from the region, he could stay.

One of the many businesses they've started over the years was one that trained women in elaborate sewing techniques. A sewing company is simple enough as a business model; it reaches a population in need—i.e., women—by giving them work with value, and it provides the kind of life-on-life ministry that is impactful. The proverbial fly in the ointment was a significant and recurrent problem among the workers. Specifically, the Muslim female employees were regularly suffering from demon possession and/or oppression.

Now, in the West, we generally don't like to talk about such things, and many of us write off anything of the like as "not real" and "unscientific." However, a significant portion of the world accepts demons and spiritual forces as part of life, an active part at that.

To fully appreciate the following story, it would be wise to take the advice Tim Keller shared in a sermon on evil, the spiritual world, and spiritual warfare. He asked his New Yorker–filled audience to suspend their fierce belief that they "know it all" for a minute and to try instead to give some credence to the 80+ percent of humanity who believe in the reality of the spiritual realm—both good and bad—and that it would be culturally narrow to do otherwise.[6]

With that in mind, consider that certain realities in Chantikland are accepted as *normal*. One particular notion is the general acceptance that Muslim women are regularly possessed by demons during their monthly cycle. The phenomenon seems like it might be just rumor because, generally, the women stay home from work during this time. Yet, one day just a couple years ago, one of James and Ayu's employees, a young Muslim girl, chose to come to work anyway.

Ayu, running a bit behind that morning, received a frantic phone call urging her to hurry into work. She bustled up to the building and saw a man yelling up at the factory windows, and what he was yelling was quite disconcerting. He screamed name after name of local demons without stop.

Ayu ran up the stairs and burst into the second-floor workroom. On the floor lay a young Muslim girl named Hati. She was writhing on the floor and foaming at the mouth, with twenty-two other employees crowding around. Through intense contortions that looked almost like seizures, Hati screamed that she was seeing demons. The Chantik, who are highly influenced by black magic and animism in addition to their Islamic adherence, began to shout for someone to run and get garlic, which according to those traditions wards off evil.

Shouting over the din, Ayu boomed out the command, "In the name of Jesus, you need to be silent, demon!"

In an instant, the employees were silenced, the girl lay still and limp on the floor, and the man outside the window ceased his venomous litany of demonic names and fled the place. In one clear moment, the employees of the sewing factory witnessed the power of Jesus Christ the Savior to set someone free.

• • •

Through the many years and the tens of thousands of lives touched by their ministry, James and Ayu have never lost sight of the message the Lord gave them in the graveyard long ago—the Easter message. The truth that Christ is the Savior who comes to seek and save the lost, and that they were called to bring that message to the Chantik. To this day, they labor toward that great end.

LESSONS LEARNED

1. Through one the Lord can bless many.
2. A prayer once prayed doesn't mean the answer will last forever, but when the Lord answers be thankful and make the most of the opportunity He's given you.
3. When the Lord is calling you to be bold on behalf of the welfare and/or salvation of others, be bold in His name.
4. When tragedy strikes, respond first and foremost with tangible expressions of Christ's love, and let that speak to the wounded in heart and health.
5. Never be afraid to innovate how you live out your example for Christ, and be ready to answer anyone who asks you about the hope you have. But do so with gentleness and respect.[7]
6. The name of Jesus is powerful. Calling upon His name will cast out both fear and demons.

Chapter 3 Citations

1. Holy Bible. New International Version. Ephesians 2:10.
2. Holy Bible. New Living Translation. Job 38:4.
3. Holy Bible. New Living Translation. Isaiah 65:24.
4. Holy Bible. New American Standard Bible. 2 Corinthians 5:20.
5. Holy Bible. New International Version. 1 Peter 3:15.
6. "Spiritual Warfare." Timothy Keller podcast. Redeemer.com, July 3, 2012. https://itunes.apple.com/us/podcast/timothy-keller-podcast/id352660924?mt=2
7. Holy Bible. New International Version. 1 Peter 3:15.

FOUR

GWEN:
THE UNCONVENTIONAL
DYNAMITE

Not all those who wander are lost.
      ~J. R. R. Tolkien, *The Fellowship of the Ring*

Whether it is Bilbo and Frodo Baggins of Tolkien's *Lord of the Rings* series or little Much Afraid in Hannah Hurnard's epic allegory *Hinds' Feet on High Places*, we have come to embrace that heroes and heroines invariably "face trials of many kinds."[1] Their paths are not smooth, nor are they straight. All too often they appear to be put off course as a result either of their own choices or the events happening around them. The truth is, however, that the author has a specific purpose for every step.

Why then are we so baffled that the Author and Perfecter of our faith,[2] the Guide to our path, will intentionally allow us to "wander" in life to gain character or compassion through our own trials? It is more than reasonable to believe that He allows us to travel through difficult lands, seasons, and circumstances in order to arrive eventually at our own great and glorious ending. We just need to remember, in the moments of worry or discouragement, that we are not lost just because our path may wander.

Gwen's Circuitous Route

Gwen went to college to study pharmacology, and through the witness of a longtime friend, Anne, she gave her life to the Lord during that time. It didn't take long to realize that Gwen was not, and never would be, a passive believer. She was an evangelist through and through.

After college, Gwen's career path started as a pharmacist for a handful of years. Then, her path turned toward the marketing side of the pharmaceutical industry for another handful of years. All the while, wherever she found herself, she was evangelizing.

Fast-forward a dozen or so years and you'd have found Gwen in her mid-thirties, still unmarried, still evangelizing, still in marketing, and invited by a friend on a short-term summer trip with New Lands mission agency. At this point in life, the Lord had beautifully shaped her to be intelligent, resourceful, adventurous, and *available*.

Jumping at the chance to go on a New Lands summer trip, Gwen, with her entrepreneurial spirit, chose a trip to Russia. The problem was that the trip to Russia was *full*. New Lands urged her to consider an amazing opportunity to take a trip a bit further east to Chantikland. What might have seemed to be a digression or "problem" in life was the Lord purposefully placing a turn in her path. He was calling her to travel down the path of His will—with a future full of adventure, boldness on behalf of Christ, and sacrifice for the sake of the Kingdom. He called Gwen to the Chantikland mission field because when you have an unusual problem, you need an unconventional solution; and she was just that.

Unconventional Dynamite

It makes sense that the Lord would redeem Saul/Paul in order to use him on behalf of His Kingdom. Paul was a "Hebrew of Hebrews," with all the advantages of birth, education, training, and position[3]—a man perfectly suited to make a powerful impact on the first generation of the church once he acknowledged Jesus Christ as Savior. The Lord, however, does not always choose such obvious leaders for His purposes. In fact, His unconventional choices always prove to be so very interesting—David the runt, Rahab the prostitute, Ruth the foreigner, Mary the virgin, Joseph the slave, and Gwen the unmarried thirty-eight-year-old pharmacist turned marketing professional.

God's unconventional choices always prove to be so very interesting.

Gwen's summer trip to Chantikland was the first domino in the long line of movements the Lord would take in her life. On it, she met Darren and Catherine as teammates and James and Ayu as team hosts. The four of them had met the previous year on the exploratory trip that launched the Chantik adoption within CHCC, and Gwen fit right in.

This trip sowed the seeds of Gwen's future. She thought the Lord was either calling her or she was having a midlife crisis! Fortunately for everyone, it was clear that this was her calling. She started praying and looking for opportunities to return to Chantikland.

Through the numerous CHCC contacts from this first trip, Gwen learned about the trip they were planning the following year through their new agency partner, the Venture Group. Granted, she wasn't a member of Cherry Hills (she had never even set foot in Colorado), but she didn't let that stop her. Her sense of call, combined with her moxie, led her to sign up for the CHCC/Venture Group trip to return to Chantikland.

As the trip grew closer, Gwen's boss grew more and more agitated that she was going. He was unrelenting in pressuring her to back out of the trip. Discouraged, she called the Venture Group; and they had an interesting solution to the problem. They suggested that she come to candidate training school instead of either going on the trip or staying with her job. That phone call cast the gates of her future wide open. Attending the training would be one more huge step away from a life of predictability and comfort and toward her calling. She agreed, consequently quit her job and went.

Gwen dove into the Venture Group's candidate school with enthusiasm. And to her surprise, she found Darren (from CHCC and her first trip) in the same class. They reconnected, and Darren shared about a business-as-mission (BAM) type of enterprise that he had in the works with James and Ayu. Upon recognizing Gwen's business acumen, he invited her to be the international director of marketing for the venture.

Gwen came home from candidate school with the adult version of a "camp high," and immediately put her house on the market. She was on fire. You'd think, with her energy and enthusiasm, that the Lord would get her to Chantikland as soon as possible. But *that* is why He is God and we are *not*!

Her house languished on the market, with no buyer interest, until she terminated the listing and sought God's will again in prayer. Gwen felt that the timing must not be right, but she still wanted to continue preparing herself to go. So, she enrolled in four classes over the course of a year to improve her knowledge of theology and the Bible.

During this time of waiting, Gwen worked the BAM venture with Darren, James, and Ayu and officially joined the CHCC Go

Team. Ultimately, the BAM endeavor faded out, but it gave her the experience with Chantikland, business, and international importing and exporting that would become the hallmark of her future work. The time was an opportunity for needed refinement and deepening of her knowledge and skills. She completed the university courses and put her house back on the market, and within four days it sold.

It was finally time. Gwen moved to Denver for six months to get to know the church in person and to prepare for the move to Chantikland. Upon arriving and getting acquainted with everyone, who do you think she discovered was on staff? None other than Anne—the friend who had introduced her to the Lord all those years before!

. . .

Waiting and delays create a playground for impatience and discouragement, but we must fight against the temptation to indulge in those unproductive and faithless activities. Longing after a life filled with purpose and calling is *good*, as it speaks of our desires (which hopefully align with God's will), but waiting is the refining process He often uses to take believers one step closer to being *great*. We don't have the omniscience to know what the Lord is putting into place or the timing that best suits His will. Instead, we must wait and place our hope where it belongs: in the One who is our Guide. Therefore, as we wait, we must trust that He wants us not just to make *a move*, but *the right move*—guided by His hands.

For Gwen, business would be, and still is, the key to unlocking opportunities for ministry in Chantikland. The Lord needed her to walk the path that she did so she'd come prepared for the life He wants for her. Consequently, it shouldn't surprise us that she is God's *unconventional dynamite*. That's right, *dynamite*. She isn't meek or cowering. She's smart, quick, and unflinching in the face of the call on her life: to share Christ, through any means, in one of the spiritually dark corners of the world.

HURDLES AND HANG-UPS

PRAYER #64: *"Pray for missionaries to effectively share the gospel with Chantik Muslims."*

Missionaries in Chantikland need to understand that the message of Christ is clouded by the centuries-old animosity the Chantik hold for Christians. Tragically, their first significant exposure to a "Christian" nation came at the hands of colonialists who subjugated them for centuries and understandably engendered tremendous bitterness. Furthermore, as a tribal people, the Chantik have always been at odds with several neighboring tribes who are culturally Christian. These other tribes enjoy freedoms that contradict Islamic law—like eating pork—and therefore the Chantik Muslims find Christians to be *disgusting* and *filthy*.

If the history of oppression wasn't enough, and the tension with neighboring tribes wasn't as significant, they would still have ample reason to confuse who Christ is with the actions of so-called Christian nations, namely *ours* (the United States). In recent years the Chantik have been exposed to our Western media, and what they see is rampant promiscuity featured in nearly every sitcom and serial drama. How can we fault them for confusing Christ, and His Kingdom, with the wanton behavior that is acceptable and even encouraged in the media of our "Christian" nation?

Collectively, the Chantik see Christians as immoral and filthy people, and they are fiercely opposed to anything that hints at subjugation. These fears are massive hurdles that all missionaries must overcome as they endeavor to live lives of moral integrity and honor, which is a significant part of their witness. Evangelism is not just walking someone through the prayer of conversion. Evangelism is every act and word that helps turn someone toward a right understanding of Jesus Christ.

Gwen is particularly keen at allaying the misperceptions of the Chantik by having them focus solely on *Christ* and not on Christians.

> # Evangelism is every act and word that helps turn someone toward a right understanding of Jesus Christ.

Once, she was riding a local transport van from one city to another in order to conduct business. The trip took the better part of the day, so it was natural that the eight passengers in the van would begin to chat quietly with each other.

Gwen struck up a conversation with the passengers behind her—a grandmother, mother (both in full burkas—the traditional Muslim garment covering women from head to toe), and the two grandchildren. When the van stopped for lunch, she asked if she could sit with them at their table. They welcomed her, and as she sat, she asked if they would excuse her for a moment while she bent her head in prayer for the meal. Gwen didn't pray aloud. She didn't take a long time, and her behavior wasn't extravagant in any way. Yet, that simple act of prayer spoke volumes to the women.

The women commented to Gwen that she must be very religious, adding that they wanted to hear about her faith. Their interest was clear, and she wanted to satisfy their curiosity. However, she wanted to do it in such a way that they could see Christ clearly despite the cultural differences and difficulties.

Gwen's first move was to avoid being pinned down by the religious title of "Christian." Instead, she sidestepped the misperceptions commonly held of Christians in that part of the world by saying she was a "follower of Jesus Christ." The result was a joyfully in-depth and explicit conversation about her conversion and relationship to Christ, as well as the plan and purpose of salvation for anyone who believes. The women were so interested that they invited her to stay the night at their in-laws' house. Though Gwen couldn't continue on with them for the night, she thanked the Lord for the opportunity to plant seeds of His truth in the seemingly fertile ground of their hearts.

• • •

These one-off moments of evangelism happen regularly, and it is our job as believers to have faith that the workers in the field will sow and water seeds of faith and that the Lord will be faithful to bring the growth (1 Cor. 3:6-7).

CARPE DIEM, WITH A SIDE OF COOKIES

PRAYER #63: *"Pray that Chantik Muslims will test Islam to see if it is really from God."*

Being a missionary is a relational affair. One relationship can lead to dozens of others, especially when you are invited to a friend's home for a holiday.

Gwen met Eri, a university student in the capital city, in the early days of her work among the Chantik. While Eri was immediately open to hearing about the gospel, over the years of their friendship she has yet to come to faith in Christ. What she did do, however, was act as a gateway to a blessed opportunity.

Seven years into their friendship, Eri invited Gwen "home" for a holiday. The home they would be going to was in the rural village where her parents still lived, deep in the interior of Chantikland. Eri is from a big family with ten siblings, all but one of which returned home during the weeklong celebration of this holiday.

To prepare for this unique opportunity, Gwen had been praying that the Lord would put in her path someone who was open to the Good News. That morning Gwen was introduced to Nevi, Eri's sister-in-law. The two women hit it off instantly.

Eri circulated among the family and left Gwen in Nevi's company. It wasn't long before Nevi started to share very personal matters; specifically, she shared with Gwen her frustrations with Islam. She had talked to the spiritual leaders about how many of the beliefs within Islam didn't seem to fit together. Particularly, she questioned why adherence to ritual was extremely important and yet what was inside a person's heart didn't seem to matter at all. Nevi poured her heart out about how discouraged she was when the leaders told her to "stop questioning" and "that she had no right to do so" and "she needed to be quiet." Nevi revealed that she isn't the only one in her community who has questions, but that others are too afraid to speak up after her rebuke and in light of the continually oppressive atmosphere in the mosque.

Gwen was blown away by the wide-open door to share the Good News of Christ. Enthusiastically, she answered every question that Nevi put to her about Jesus, and they talked all morning. Nevi was thrilled about what she was hearing, and when the time was nearing for her and her husband to leave, Gwen offered to give her some books she'd brought along that would answer more of her questions about Jesus. Wanting the books very much, but not knowing how to get them from Gwen in a room full of Muslims who all know that proselytizing can be punishable by death under shari'a law, Nevi cleverly asked, "Now where is the gift you had for me?"

Picking up on the cue, Gwen ran to her luggage and found a small bag where she put the books in the bottom and a package of cookies sticking out of the top. Gwen handed over the gift, and both women smiled and hugged, knowing the gift was much sweeter than cookies.

LABORERS FOR THE HARVEST

PRAYER #67: *"God knows the future for the Chantik church, which will be established one day. Pray for His will to be done."*

While the Chantik have always been the focus of Gwen's ministry, technically, she only lived in the region for about six months early in her sojourn as a missionary. She has spent months at a time there over the last nineteen years, but primarily she has lived in major cities near Chantikland.

From the very beginning, Gwen realized her gifts required living in a larger city than any of those found in Chantikland. After those six months, the Lord moved her just outside of the region and into a large city, which acts as one of several international shipping hubs in the region. There she could easily conduct the importing and exporting that was part of many of her business-as-mission efforts.

Another virtue of living outside of Chantikland was that it gave Gwen a unique opportunity to marry her business savvy with her desire to see a church-planting movement take root among the Chantik. She and a Christian associate and friend, Ankur, started a ministry training school, which was actually legal to do in this city just outside of Chantikland. The goal was to train up a generation of graduates and launch many of them into Chantikland with church-planting hopes.

Gwen and Ankur specifically recruited from other tribes from the same country with the thought that they could blend into Chantik society better than any blond-haired, blue-eyed foreigner. The Lord blessed the endeavor, and soon the recruiting extended beyond even those tribes to include expats from countries around the hemisphere.

The school grew from six students the first year to twenty-eight students the second year. At that point, Gwen turned the school over to local Christian leaders. Empowering nationals was the focus of the new initiative through CHCC, and the time was right for her to pass the torch of the training center on to local leaders she knew and trusted.

Since then the center has continued to thrive, and nearly a decade's worth of graduates have come from it, many of whom still have a Chantik focus. In fact, Gwen came to the training organization several years later when a sudden opportunity opened up in Chantikland. She recruited ten of the church-planting/disciple-making trained students into roles as community organizers to serve a community in the north that was in desperate need after a massive natural disaster. A number of those original community organizers are still in Chantikland a decade later, working and ministering in the communities.

GATHERING TOGETHER

PRAYER #20: *"Thank God for assembling different ethnic peoples . . . and for the opportunity to influence other peoples from that starting point."*

A few years into Gwen's ministry, she heard about and attended a conference of believers in the southern region of the country. Handfuls of the tribes in that part of the region were known to be Christian, and the opportunity to network with and be refreshed by the company of other Christians wasn't something she was going to pass up.

At the conference, five people groups in the country were chosen for focused prayer, the Chantik among them. As they broke into small groups, Gwen enthusiastically went to the group praying for the Chantik. She joined with eight others, and during that time the Lord sparked a vision.

The vision was to build on the momentum of prayer for the Chantik at this conference by hosting the same conference in the border town to Chantikland. This would be an opportunity to unify the believers right there in the neighboring region with a collective vision to minister to and among the Chantik and to link them with those from other areas who were already passionately doing so. Gwen approached the leader of the conference with the idea; and, to her surprise, he said that she was an *answer to prayer*. For some time he had been asking the Lord to provide someone who would be willing to host a conference in that region.

It took a year of blood, sweat, and tears to put it together, but the time was finally upon her. The conference had been planned and promoted by a group of nationals connected to the overseeing organization of the conference and by Gwen through her networks. Though there are always differences in opinions, methods, and motivations, the conference by all accounts was a raging success. Nearly four hundred believers gathered together, seventy of which were specifically dedicated to focused prayer for the Chantik during and after the conference.

The efforts and diligence of those seventy individuals have been blessed. They started and still run many of the ongoing efforts among the Chantik. Jesus tells believers in Matthew 18:19-20 that if two (or more) of us agree about anything we ask God for, our heavenly Father will be faithful to fulfill it. The conference attendees prayed for the salvation of the Chantik through Christ; and even now, fifteen or twenty years later, the Lord is honoring that agreement through pockets of believers being discovered and/or created.

To say that the work among the Chantik is challenging is a gross understatement, but it is worth it to share with them the hope of salvation. Specifically, the two messages of Scripture that seem to ring the loudest among the Chantik are *the reality of unconditional love* and *the security of salvation* before God through Jesus. These virtues of Christianity are entirely new to them because neither animism nor Islam—the two religions that have long held precedence in Chantikland—offer such eternal expressions of loving-kindness.

A PLANE RIDE TO HOPE

PRAYER #60: *"Pray against the resignation to spiritual nonunderstanding and spiritual poverty, which is so common among the Muslim Chantik. Ask for the Holy Spirit to stir them with a hunger to know the truth through questioning Islam."*

On the return flight from one of Gwen's business trips to Chantikland, she found herself boarding the plane on the first day of Ramadan (the Islamic month of fasting). With the exception of herself, the rest of the passengers were Chantik, and entirely men, as far as she could see over the rows. This was the last situation she would have imagined for an opportunity to witness to arise—and yet, *it did*.

Gwen took her seat next to a man reading a newspaper. The front page of the paper had a huge article about Ramadan, and in a glance, she noticed the word *cleansing* written in a headline. Gwen being Gwen, she asked to borrow the paper when the man was finished because she wanted to know what Ramadan was supposed to cleanse you from. The Chantik are very generous and the man had already begun handing her the paper as she made the request. However, when she mentioned cleansing, he grabbed it back and began searching the article.

His response was simple, and very telling. "I don't know; it doesn't say," he said, sounding discouraged.

At this point, other ears had perked up. The man's agitation over not understanding the actual purpose or point of a season he faithfully adhered to made him uncommonly loud on the midsized plane. He turned to the man on his other side and asked him. That man didn't know either. Gwen's seatmate was distraught by this.

Salvation isn't based on human effort.

Gently but boldly, Gwen pressed forward into the conversation and began to share why people need cleansing. She started with Genesis and the reality of sin. She explained its stranglehold on our lives and that it comes with a death sentence. She told him about God's redeeming love, which is consistent and faithful and *not* based on our actions or good works. She spoke the truth of Ephesians 2:8-9:

> *For by grace you have been saved through faith, and that not of yourselves; it is the gift of God, not of works, lest anyone should boast.* (NKJV)

Gwen had a captive and attentive audience. In this all-male, all-Muslim plane, everyone within earshot was silent and focused on what she was about to say. In the most thorough fashion possible, she shared the length and breadth of Scripture, as well as the plan and purpose of salvation in Christ. She was explicit in sharing about Jesus and how salvation through Him isn't based on any human effort. You don't have to be good enough, obedient enough, religious enough; rather it is God's redemptive and loving nature that prompted Him to reconcile to Himself a sinful and rebellious people. And, He did it because of His great love for us.

Her seatmate was so moved hearing about a God who could love him, in his sin, that he invited Gwen to share this hope with his whole family. He needed them to know as well.

Gwen very much wanted to follow up with his family, but this experience happened shortly after the natural disaster, so communication within Chantikland was even more difficult than normal due to downed cell towers, etc. They were never able to reconnect, but on that day, the truth was both *spoken* and *heard*. In that moment, on that plane, dozens of Chantik men heard the truth of Christ and His unconditional love for them.

HARD PRESSED

PRAYER #26: *"Pray for great courage for new Christians. They will possibly face rejection and persecution from families and village communities."*

The work of translating the Bible into any local language is a long and arduous endeavor, but the payoff is eternal. While the endeavor does have a monetary price, respectively it's insignificant. Rather, it is the price to distribute or own the Bibles that is *so* costly. In Chantikland, that price could be your life—at least, life as you know it.

Converts to Christianity have had to flee their villages, their families, and sometimes the law of the land. This persecution, which comes in varying degrees of severity, is often doled out based on owning a Bible. It is one of the tangible pieces of "evidence" used to point to conversion or the attempt to convert someone else, all of which is a crime in Chantikland.

The government recognizes only six official religions, and all citizens have their religion listed on their government identification card. Whether you practice or not, you are registered as Hindu, Buddhist, Catholic, Protestant, Confucianist, or Muslim. Registered Christians *are* allowed to possess Bibles. The difficulty is that you are not allowed to publicly display possession of one, though you can read one in your home. You are not, however, permitted to read the Bible aloud anywhere, even in private, in case a Muslim might overhear you. To give a Bible to a Muslim could be fatal if you are reported—and, at the least, is grounds for imprisonment. That is why it was so significant that Gwen met Saadi, a Chantik former Muslim turned avid Christian.

BIBLES IN THEIR HANDS

PRAYER #21: *"Ask God to raise up influential Muslim converts who can return to their place of origin to report that they have met the Savior."*

Saadi was a man on a mission to distribute Bibles to any interested Chantik person. His home base was the border town where Gwen lived, but he traveled into Chantikland several times a month, boldly sharing the Good News of Christ with those who expressed interest. He had cultivated pockets of seekers over months of faithful and brave evangelism.

**• 100s • 100s • 100s •
OF BIBLES GIVEN AWAY**

Gwen wanted to support Saadi's ministry. He was gaining access that was divine. She managed to get one hundred Bibles printed in the Chantiks' language to Saadi. And, with the Lord as his guard, he distributed them up and down the province to the seekers.

Upon his return, Saadi happily reported to Gwen that seventy of the Bibles had been given to eager Chantik Muslims. The other thirty were distributed among individuals from the other religious minorities in the region. He had even written down the names of all those who took a copy to share with Gwen for prayer.

• • •

We know the Lord desires to seek and save the lost and that He is the ultimate Gardener who can produce growth within the many seeds planted. Therefore, it is important both to celebrate this success and trust in Isaiah's prophetic words from the Lord:

It is the same with my word.

I send it out, and it always produces fruit.

It will accomplish all I want it to,

and it will prosper everywhere I send it.

(Isaiah 55:11, NLT*)*

THIS LITTLE LIGHT OF MINE

PRAYER #68: *"Pray that God would call to Himself men who are leaders in their families and communities, that those who [taught] Islam would teach salvation by faith in Christ instead."*

One year during Holy Week, a Chantik friend named Ita came to visit Gwen in the border town of Chantikland where she lived. Ita knew of Gwen's faith in Jesus and cautiously accepted the invitation to attend a Good Friday service (which was allowed outside of Chantikland). But the service was a good distance from Gwen's home, and she didn't have a car to get them there. Every problem, however, is merely another opportunity for the Lord to work.

Gwen called a wealthy business contact and friend, who had a car, and asked for a ride to church. The man showed up with his car and driver and took the women to the service. Ita was quiet during the service, but clearly attentive to what she was hearing. In the car on the way home from church, Gwen asked the man—a former Muslim—to share with Ita what he had recently told her.

The man lit up, and he could barely contain his enthusiasm as he shared how he came to know Jesus and what the Lord had done in his life since. Ita couldn't believe it. She grilled him with one question after another. She was convinced this man had been forced to convert to Christianity, and even said as much to him. The man told her with confidence that it was the Lord who drew him to Himself.

His honest and bold declaration of faith prompted a shift in Ita's questions. She got to thinking about the consequences of such a faith and asked a number of questions about his family and how they reacted. He shared extensively that the love of Christ was worth the cost.

This opportunity to have a deep and honest conversation was divinely inspired, as this former Muslim shared his faith in Jesus with a current Muslim. And, it all came about because Gwen didn't have a car! Praise God for some of the little difficulties that open up extraordinary doors.

GOLDILOCKS KEPT ON MOVING

PRAYER #54: *"Long-term visas are necessary in order to live and work among the Chantik. Pray that the process of obtaining visas from the Chantik government will be easy and smooth."*

In life, we hope for the *ideal* and live with the *real*. While we would hope that every one of our missionaries (and all missionaries) would receive long-term visas to provide a sense of stability in their work and situation and to free them up to think about other things, that often isn't the case. The Lord tells us to hope in Him, not *in* our security or even *for* it. Instead, we are supposed to trust that He is directing our steps. Gwen continues to trust the Lord even though the type of visa she has been able to acquire is anything but long-term. Each visa lasts for one year; however, the kicker is that she must leave the country every sixty days. That's right, she has to leave the country every sixty days—and she's done it for the last nineteen years!

She had to leave the country and come back in, every sixty days, for seventeen years!

Fortunately, Gwen has become incredibly adept at this whole system and knows when to schedule some of her importing/exporting trips, trips back to the States, and when to go through the turnstile and "leave" the country only to join the line on the other side of the room and walk right back in. While the requirement to leave the country is a massive inconvenience, think about it—for nineteen years she has never failed to get a visa to come back. Praise God for working that out.

• • •

After all this time, Gwen's heart for the Chantik is just as passionate as ever. She is now in her sixties, but still vibrant; and after her itinerant nineteen years abroad, she is transitioning to a new phase of ministry. Her time is spent primarily stateside now, setting up and training teams in her organization with the purpose of ministering to refugees, immigrants, and even international student populations in the US. No matter where Gwen is, she'll be sharing the love of Christ with the people of the world.

LESSONS LEARNED

1. Never discount the power and focus of a single person dedicated to the Lord's work.
2. You are never too old to become a missionary.
3. God honors unity among believers with heavenly favor.
4. Be bold to share the love of Christ in both actions and words, and temper all with gentleness and respect.

Chapter 4 Citations

1. Holy Bible. New International Version. James 1:2b.
2. Holy Bible. New American Standard Bible. Hebrews 12:2.
3. Holy Bible. New International Version. Philippians 3:3-10.

FIVE

THE QUIET PERSISTENCE OF KATHY

For by the grace given me I say to every one of you:
Do not think of yourself more highly than you ought,
but rather think of yourself with sober judgment,
in accordance with the faith God has distributed
to each of you. For just as each of us has one body with
many members, and these members do not all have the same
function, so in Christ we, though many, form one body,
and each member belongs to all the others. We have different
gifts, according to the grace given to each of us.

~ Romans 12:3-6 (NIV)

Many might think that only bold personalities are fit for missionary work—people who are natural leaders and who possess the gift of evangelism and fearlessness as defining characteristics. *Not true.* At least, not all the time. The Lord has the ultimate perspective of what needs to be done to accomplish His will, and consequently He made *many members with different gifts* to see to their part of His grand plan.

Kathy is different than all the other missionaries in this book. She's an introvert. Generally, she is more quiet than flashy; she's not typically the person you would find taking command of center stage or calling attention to herself. What she is, however, is *invaluable*.

Kathy is faithful, focused, humble, dedicated, and sincere. She has the capacity to be fully dedicated to a task that isn't quickly accomplished—and *that* is rare indeed. Ultimately, her personality was very well suited for the work the Lord would do through her during her nearly nine-year tenure among the Chantik.

Her Beginning

Kathy found Christ as a sophomore in college; and just a couple years later, as she attended CHCC and participated in the church's yearly mission festival, she approached Pastor G. and said, "I think I want to be a missionary, but I don't know what one is or what they do." He immediately pointed her to the Perspectives class, which was being hosted at the church. It was the perfect place for Kathy to gain more information, training, and vision for missions. That simple little conversation would kick-start the next fifteen years of dedication to missions and evangelism in her life.

Before you knew it, Kathy had attended the class, caught the vision, and committed to a yearlong medical mission assignment in Africa. Her motivation to go was straightforward: "I needed to see that my experience of the LORD was real, that He was real, and that He was working all over the world."

Hebrews 11:6 (NIV) says, "Without faith it is impossible to please God, because anyone who comes to him must believe that he exists and that he rewards those who earnestly seek him." Kathy was certainly seeking God, and she soon saw His work in the lives of those far outside of the suburban church she was used to.

In Africa, she found herself involved in a range of activities from counting out pills in the pharmacy to working in a leprosy camp teaching the patients exercises to improve the use of their paralyzed, and possibly nerve-damaged, hands and feet. Overall, she spent six months in Niger and then six months in Burkina Faso. Unfortunately, because French is the official language of both countries, and that isn't Kathy's second language, connecting with others was a struggle. Being an introvert who didn't know the language and had difficulty finding her place in the team as a "short-termer" made for a very lonely season.

The time in Africa was by no means a waste; Kathy was doing good work. It just wasn't the great mission work that she thought she had come to do, specifically because these groups were already well evangelized. The whole experience made her seriously question if she was meant to be a missionary.

A Calling Renewed

After fulfilling her one-year commitment, Kathy came home to Denver and Cherry Hills Community Church. The time in Africa had been hard, yet she still had a heart to reach the nations for Christ. As Kathy settled back into community life at CHCC, she got caught up in the fervor of the adoption of the Chantik. There were presentations, announcements, events, fliers, pamphlets, the prayer guide, and fund-raising teams everywhere you looked. The church's enthusiasm prompted her to want to be involved, and she had the perfect opportunity to do so on the newly formed Chantik Home Team.

Joining the Home Team—*that* was the spark. The team consisted of a dozen enthusiasts, including Tim and Sandy (chapter 6), Darren (chapter 2) and his wife, and several other future members of the Go

Team. This team was passionate about moving the church along in their adoption of the Chantik. Kathy's heart swelled with the energy of the movement. Though the Go Team had not yet been officially formed, the makings of it were beginning to come together.

Kathy was invited to be a part of the next short-term trip to Chantikland. The primary focus of the trip was to pray for the people. The team met with their ministry partners, James and Ayu, and with numerous locals as they traveled from village to village.

In her late twenties at the time, Kathy happened to meet and connect with a Chantik woman around the same age. Kathy and Milli became fast friends, both on the trip and after. They struck up a pen-pal relationship, sending letters across the seas (before email). The depth and beauty of their friendship further entwined Kathy's heart with the people of Chantikland. Between the relationship with Milli and the positive experience on the trip with several others who were seriously considering joining the Go Team, Kathy had a renewed determination that she *could* be a missionary on the field—and that she *wanted* to be one.

In Africa she had struggled with intense loneliness and a lack of connection with her team, as well as an inability to connect with the locals due to the language barrier. But everything about her experience with the Chantik was different. She had already made a connection in what would turn out to be a lifelong friendship with Milli. She felt the Chantiks' spiritual need as an unreached people group, and she could imagine ways in which she could contribute to a team like the one CHCC was in the beginning stages of forming. It seemed that all the obstacles of her former experience on the field were being overcome in this new calling.

Diving In

Within a short time after the trip, Kathy committed to be a part of the CHCC Go Team. The next two years were filled with raising funds, completing candidate school, and having strategic meetings with the Go Team prior to departure. Kathy also took time to attend seminary. She wanted to refine her knowledge and further prepare herself for the field.

As the fourth Go Team member to go in-country, Kathy joined the others in a major city in Chantikland's nation. This city is home to a language school designed for missionary language acquisition. CHCC and the Venture Group both agreed that time in language school was paramount for the future of the ministry. They believed that going through the coursework at the school would provide two distinct benefits.

An obvious benefit is that formal education in the language would allow them to become proficient quicker—a necessity to communicate with those in remote parts of Chantikland, where English is less likely to be spoken. And, the less obvious benefit of spending the first year or so in language school was that team members could go through the major stages of culture shock away from the stressors of daily ministry, while using the time to bond. To some degree or another, each Go Team member attended language school.

> The first years for any missionary are about figuring it out, getting your bearings, and making connections.

After roughly a year and a half in language school, Kathy moved to the capital city of Chantikland with Gwen (chapter 4) and Tim and Sandy (chapter 6). The first years for any missionary are about figuring it out, getting your bearings, and making connections. During this time, Kathy enjoyed a number of standout ministry opportunities and encounters through her primary role on the field as an English teacher, the role for which she was initially granted a visa.

In fact, the organization that sponsored her visa also sponsored Tim and Sandy (of chapter 6). James, Ayu, and Andrew (from chapter 3) had created this organization, English Around the World, several years before; and EAW had been able to get dozens of missionaries in the country at that point. Kathy experienced daily opportunities to witness through being a living example of Christ in word and especially in deed. What you *did* rather than what you *said* tended to be a much more powerful example among the Chantik.

Kathy experienced daily opportunities to witness through being a living example of Christ in word and especially in deed.

A "Filthy" People No More

With Kathy's move to Chantikland came an unexpected challenge in the form of finding a place to live. She found a great place that suited her needs well; but when she approached the landlord, Kathy ran into the first of many instances where her morality was questioned. The questions weren't a result of anything she'd done, rather just because of who she was—a single, thirty-something woman who was an American and a Christian. All of these factors were greatly concerning to the landlord, a Muslim woman named Diya.

While Kathy's marital status was confusing to Diya—to be thirty and unmarried was unthinkable—that wasn't the biggest issue. The two worst things that Kathy could be were *Christian* and *American*.

The Chantik considered both groups to be highly immoral people.

Diya's impression of Americans was based on what she saw on TV, which showed lots of drinking, miniskirts, and rampant sexual promiscuity. (And this was her impression *before* the creation of reality TV.) Her ill will toward Christians was fed by modern examples from TV being broadcast from our "Christian nation," but it was founded on generations of tension with a neighboring tribe who was known to be largely Christian. The Chantik considered these Christians *filthy* people because they ate pork, didn't wear head coverings, and did other things that are forbidden within Islam.

Everything about Kathy was a red flag to this woman, and yet she chose to rent to her anyway. Amid the day-in-and-day-out scrutiny of her landlord, Kathy lived a consistent example of a modest, honest, and kind tenant. Her living testimony opened up lines of communication and conversation with Diya about Christ that likely wouldn't have happened otherwise. Eventually, Diya conceded that not all Christians were *filthy people*, which was a significant concession considering her former vehemence. Kathy counted the constant need to clear away misconceptions about Christianity part of her job as an ambassador of Christ—and one of the most consistent requirements of her in the field.

· · ·

Such an unassuming woman, who was unique among her team, Kathy would work her way into the hearts of the Chantik through her authenticity and kindness. Her evangelism, more often than not, was subtle. When the Spirit prompted, she'd use words to share the love of Christ; but in a culture that valued behavior and deeds far more, it was her everyday witness of modesty, kindness, and generosity that spread the aroma of Christ, encouraging a hunger for the Truth.

FROM TOP TO BOTTOM

PRAYER #44: *"Pray for teachers in high schools and universities—that the influence they have on the younger generation might be redeemed and used by God to reveal His truth."*

The English Around the World staff had a specific way of working in Chantikland. They taught conversational English to the teachers of English. Their acceptance into the school system was both wide, spanning numerous counties, and enthusiastic. In fact, the school officials wanted the work of the EAW workers to build friendships beyond the classroom with all the English teachers in their schools. The thought was that these authorized friendships would improve the pronunciation and fluency of the teachers and ultimately benefit the students.

Kathy and her Southern Baptist colleague through EAW were placed in the best high school in the entire province. It was in the capital city, and because it was the best, the principal had significant influence. This principal was so optimistic about the program that he didn't just have his English teachers come to the classes; he had *all* his high school teachers attend the classes.

Kathy's work within the EAW program answered prayers in two major ways. The first was among the upper levels of administration in the school system and within high levels of the government. Specifically, the enthusiastic principal, who was very well connected and anxious to improve his own command of English, came to the classes along with his teachers. As a result of being so pleased by what he and his teachers were learning (and because of the Lord's favor), he invited Kathy and her colleagues to a gathering at the governor's house. His influence was extensive, so invitations to gatherings like these and others opened up uncommon access to high-level officials in all different aspects of the government. Kathy and her colleagues hoped that with each positive encounter with officials they met, openness to Christians and Christianity would be increased.

The second way that prayers were answered was in working with the teachers themselves. The precedent that the principal had set was a wide-open door of access to build relationships. Kathy and her colleagues took the teachers out to dinner, went to the beach with them, and just hung out with them so they could talk, talk, and talk some more. This regular interaction gave Kathy and the rest the perfect platform to build relationships with substance. It didn't take more than a couple meetings before all of the niceties in casual conversation were out of the way, thereby freeing up time to talk about real things, and eternal things, when the Spirit prompted.

Because the region of Chantikland was so insulated from the rest of the world—both by its primitive infrastructure and Islamic law—the majority of the population was without access to huge swaths of information that would be common to a nation with more global access to information. This gap in knowledge worked in the favor of Kathy and her colleagues as they built relationships with the teachers. They could share a story from the Bible to communicate some truth and it would fall on completely fresh ears.

A practice that the EAW workers, Kathy included, would use regularly was to choose one Bible story a week to work into conversation—be it a story or parable from the Old or New Testament. Generally, the stories were focused on themes of morality or justice or illustrated what Christians are like—that is, what they value. These snippets from the Bible helped break down misperceptions about Christianity and breed curiosity about Christ.

Almost without exception, the Chantik teachers had never heard anything like the weekly stories shared. Some responded with enthusiasm, interest, and lots of questions; others with skepticism.

One of the Scripture passages that Kathy used on a regular basis was the parable of the prodigal son in Luke 15. It was perfect for communicating the universal truth that we are all sinners who need to be saved and can be saved by grace, not by works. It beautifully illustrates that salvation and love are gifts from God, a theme contrary to both their animistic and Islamic understandings of God.

One time, Kathy was able to share the prodigal son parable with a religion educator of the highest level in the school system. His heartbreaking response to the father's actions in the passage was, "I'm not sure that kind of love exists." He simply couldn't fathom a father—or more to the point, a God—who would welcome home an errant, sinful child with love and acceptance. He admitted to having no frame of reference for that from what he taught from Islam, and tragically his conclusion was that it must not exist.

> His heartbreaking response to the actions of the prodigal son's father was, "I'm not sure that kind of love exists."

However closed or hopeless some individuals seemed, the Lord used the EAW program to impact countless students, as teachers would return to their classes and share the stories they'd heard. With every gospel-laden story told, a crack in the bedrock of Islam was created. In the Lord's time, and by His will, the fertile ground in the hearts of the Chantik with ears to hear will be found.

SEEDS, SEEDS, EVERYWHERE SEEDS

PRAYER #49: *"Pray that God would raise up Christians who desire to share the gospel of Jesus while teaching English to avid, Chantik learners."*

After building numerous relationships through EAW, Kathy and her colleagues threw a Christmas party for their teacher friends. To their great surprise, twenty-seven people showed up for the party. With an opportunity like that, they plunged forward with boldness. The night started with all the typical socializing and frivolity; but at the right moment, Kathy and the others shifted the focus of the party by putting on a film about Jesus' life, from His birth to the Sermon on the Mount.

Unsure of what to expect, Kathy watched the crowd as they watched the movie. Each partygoer was fully engaged. There was a blessed sense of concentration as the film unfolded, so much so that she saw a sea of nodding heads as they took in the message of the film. This Christmas party turned out to be a divine moment to communicate about Christ, and without a doubt, seeds of truth were sewn.

We are called to be "sowers of seed" wherever we go. Even Jesus acknowledged the disheartening reality that some seed will fall among the rocks and will wither; some seed will fall on the path, only to be trampled; and some seed will fall among thorns, where it will be choked out. It is the final location where some seed will fall that should give us hope and joy in sowing seed to begin with—the good soil. The Lord tells us in the parable that the good soil produces a crop of a "hundred, sixty or thirty times what was sown" (Matthew 13:23, NIV).

So, while we don't know who, if any, of those specific partygoers came to know the Lord, we do know that if any one of them are "good soil," then we can count on the Father to bring an impressive return from that one little seed sown that night.

THE ODD SHEEP

PRAYER #10: *"Pray that the Chantik people would know Jesus as their only Hope and Savior."*

As trust between Kathy and the teachers grew, they increasingly felt free to share what they believed with her. She encouraged them to share openly, because it allowed her to share on deeper levels in return. Depending on the source, however, some of what she heard was less than pleasant to endure. Particularly, any comments that came from a thick-bearded, seemingly radical man named Muhammad.

Week after week, Muhammad showed up at both the classes and social occasions prepared to badger Kathy. He took great pleasure in challenging her at every turn. He brought her books about Islam, and he was relentless in criticizing her for not being married. He adamantly advocated for all things Islam, so much so that she wondered if he was a part of the rebel cause in the civil war, advocating for shari'a law among other things. It was enough to wonder if he was a *lost cause.*

Then, one day after a particularly difficult encounter with Muhammad in class, Kathy and all the teachers were walking out of the class when Muhammad asked in front of the whole group if Kathy would give him a ride to the mechanic's shop down the street. Kathy froze. It would be completely inappropriate under normal circumstances for her to be alone in a car with a man. More shocking still was to be asked to do that very thing by a man who constantly harangued her about Muslim morality.

The man pleaded with the group that it was just down the street, and Kathy hesitantly said that she would be willing if he really needed a ride and if it was acceptable to the other teachers. The whole group of teachers began discussing the situation and eventually decided that it would be OK since it was such a short distance.

Completely unaware of what to expect next, Kathy slid into the car praying ardently. The man climbed into the passenger seat; and as soon as he shut the door, everything about him changed. Gone was the belligerent radical she knew, and next to her sat a man pleading with her to give him a Bible. Muhammad confessed that prior to working in this school in the capital, he was in another region learning from another EAW teacher, a Southern Baptist. This other teacher would tell him Bible stories night after night, and he *had* to know more. He begged her to find another male mentor for him to meet with and for a Bible that he could keep and continue reading on his own.

The whole time that Muhammad was putting up such a fierce front of adherence to Islam in Kathy's classes, he was just waiting for the right moment to confess the truth to her—that he was desperate to hear more about the saving grace of Jesus. He acted the way he did publicly because he was afraid.

> He sat next to her pleading for a Bible.

The civil war was reaching a fever pitch, and both sides were growing increasingly violent. Publicly pursuing Christ at that point would have meant death, but Muhammad's desire to know more was greater. That's why he risked this clandestine meeting with Kathy to make his request for a Bible.

Muhammad's revelation to Kathy came just weeks before all Westerners were kicked out of the region by the government due to the violence in the civil war. Consequently, she wasn't able to connect him with ongoing male mentorship; but she *was* able to slip him portions of the Bible that had been translated into one of his native languages. Pray that Muhammad's desire for Christ continues to flourish in the light of the Word he *did* receive.

GOD FOUND HIM. THEN HE FOUND GOD.

PRAYER #18: *"Praise the Lord for His searching love, which extends to every human being. May He redeem the desires of Muslims who are honestly pursuing the Truth. Ask for their fasting and searching to be met with the truth of Jesus Christ."*

One particular gift Kathy possesses is the ability to see the Lord moving around her and through the work of brothers and sisters in Christ. You'd hear her say again and again, "We just kept running into what the Lord was doing all the time." This sentiment is particularly true with the story of Mul.

Mul, as a young Chantik man, had been sent out into the world to "make his fortune" in order to be able to marry his betrothed. Unfortunately, fortunes weren't easy to come by in his poor rural village, so off he went to a larger city in Chantikland to find a job at a recycling plant. Long days of hard work had him sorting through countless scraps of paper.

One day, out of the deep mounds of paper before him, a scrap of paper caught Mul's eye; and on it he read: "'For I know the plans I have for you,' declares the Lord, 'plans to prosper you and not to harm you, plans to give you hope and a future'" (Jeremiah 29:11, NIV). Stunned by what he read, he secreted the scrap into his pocket for safekeeping. He had to know more. Day after day, Mul went back to work scouring the piles for anything else like what he'd found, and the Lord blessed his searching. He found verse after verse mentioning Jesus and salvation, and with these scraps of hope, his desire to know more grew exponentially.

Mul moved to the border city just outside of Chantikland. At this point, after having found a number of verses in the recycled paper piles, he knew he was looking for the Jesus of Christianity. He did what seemed completely reasonable; now that he lived in the border town, where there was more freedom to talk about Christianity, he approached fellow countrymen who were Christians to ask questions. Unfortunately, because of the violent reputation of the Chantik—specifically, as ardent Muslims engaging in a civil war, which was in part motivated by the desire to practice more extreme Islamic law—the Christians he questioned literally ran from him in fear. Seeking answers, Mul went to a church, but he was thrown out for fear that he was a spy. Through all this, he kept searching.

Eventually, someone was willing to give Mul a Bible; and with that gesture, his eternal thirst was quenched in one night, as he read the Scriptures cover to cover. In his room, alone but for the presence of the Almighty, Mul—a full-blooded Chantik man—gave his life to the Lord.

Mul reached out again to various Christians and shared about his conversion. Ultimately, he became an integral part of the growing network of Christian workers in the border town who were focused on sharing Christ with the Chantik. He contributed greatly and had exceptional insight, given that he knew what they would have to go through to become believers in Jesus.

Kathy met Mul among this network of believers, and the way that the Lord found him confirmed to her that the Lord was working in ways beyond their comprehension. She knew that they needed to keep praying, seeking, and trusting the Lord to do His will among the Chantik.

A LONG TIME IN COMING

PRAYER #9: *"God longs for the Chantik people to know Him. Pray that those who seek God will find Him, whether that be through dreams or visions or the testimony of believers."*

Every Christian has their own unique story of how they found Christ. Like Paul, some believers experience a "Damascus road" type of conversion, where the Lord meets them in a moment and they immediately accept Him and begin following Him. Countless others, however, walk a slow and complicated path to Christ—a path involving many years and numerous stages of surrender and sacrifice. Choosing to walk on any path that leads to Jesus requires sacrifice. And, given that He is the ultimate Guide to our paths, it is safe to say that He knows which one we *need* to travel in order to reach Him.

It is that second path, the slower one with many turns, that the Lord called Lani to walk. Lani was a woman connected to several of the Go Team members, but none more so than Kathy.

The Go Team met Lani not long after they moved into Chantikland. They were all still trying to understand the spiritual landscape amid the civil war raging around them. Lani was a difficult person to comprehend. She had such violent mood swings that it was likely she either had an undiagnosed mental illness, possibly bipolar disorder, or was possessed by an evil spirit, which was a distinct possibility in a region known for its practice of black magic. In fact, people routinely summon an evil spirit upon someone they don't like.

Kathy watched Lani gravitate to them in all her mental states— suicidal at times, clingy in one moment, and then belligerent and vexed in the next. Lani went through phases of being very curious and then distant, repeating this cycle again and again over the course of years. In response to Lani's questions or to the promptings of the

Holy Spirit, Kathy had shared with her the Good News of salvation in Christ a number of times and in a variety of ways. She'd even gotten Lani a Bible, and together they'd read through numerous passages. Lani had searched the Scriptures on her own as well.

In those first years, Lani wasn't ready to move past curiosity to acceptance, but she was definitely attracted to the message of the gospel. She was of marriageable age in Chantikland, and consequently the uniqueness of the Bible's perspective on the value of women resonated with her. She was so taken by the picture of unity and love in a biblical marriage that she pleaded for those verses to be a part of not only her marriage ceremony to her Muslim fiancé, but a part of their marriage. Her fiancé responded with an ultimatum—she had to stop reading the Bible and abandon this pursuit of Christ, or the engagement was off. Lani did the unthinkable in Chantikland: she canceled the engagement. She would not abandon her pursuit of Christ. This may not have been a proclamation of faith as we in the Western world traditionally think of it, but what else is it when someone chooses to follow Christ despite the cost?

With the engagement canceled and her family aware of why, her mother, from her deathbed, begged Lani not to change religions. This request from her mother warred within Lani, because at the same time the heavenly Father was asking for the same allegiance from her—His daughter, whom He loved.

Torn over her spiritual destiny, she went to the beach to look out upon the ocean. She had both a Bible and the Quran with her. At this point, she had what can only be described as a waking dream or a vision of herself with a foot in each spiritual world. Lani explained later that she knew in an instant that one path led to death and the other path led to life; and in that moment Jesus appeared to her and said, "Come to Me, all who are weary and heavy-laden, and I will give you rest."[1] Right there, on the beach, alone but for the presence of the

Almighty, she gave her life to the Lord!

Kathy and Lani did not always live close to one another, because at one point Kathy was forced to leave the region because the civil war was escalating dangerously and the government forced foreigners to leave. However, the distance didn't matter. They kept in touch, and when Kathy returned to Chantikland she found Lani leading a Bible study with another woman. Kathy looked on with amazement at this transformed woman. Salvation hadn't eradicated all of her mental issues. But overall, Lani radiated a sense of peace that passed all understanding, and her faith was growing exponentially.

Lani reached out to Kathy a couple years ago to share one final piece of good news. Though Kathy has been back in the United States for a handful of years, their friendship has continued, and the news was too good for Lani not to share with Kathy. Lani was at last ready to be baptized in the name of Jesus.

This decision was so much more than just a Sunday morning dip before friends. A Muslim who gets baptized into another faith is subject to punishment by death in Chantikland; and therefore, baptism is the ultimate sign of conversion. Lani's willingness to take a step of obedience to Christ that could cost her life was, and is, a beautiful act of sacrifice and surrender. Together the women reveled in both the cost of discipleship and the riches of salvation as they celebrated Lani's baptism.

Altogether, from the time she first heard about Christ, it took six years for Lani to profess faith on that beach and thirteen years for her to be baptized. We look at this lengthy courtship of salvation as a long time in coming, but what is more important—*the speed at which a seed takes root* or *the soil in which it is planted*? Though her heart took years and years of tilling, in the end it was made into good soil, and from it the Lord has already begun the work of producing a secondary harvest. Lani's willingness to share the love of Christ with others will bear fruit, in God's timing and through patient discipleship and reading the Scriptures—just like Kathy did with her.

THE HELPERS WERE HELPED

PRAYER #47: *"As the younger generations struggle with finding their own identity, pray they would find it in the Lord Jesus Christ."*

If necessity is the mother of invention, then entrepreneurialism is the father of visas. Or at least that's what Kathy was hoping when she, like countless other missionaries, found herself in need of another visa. It happens all the time—the opportunity that had secured her visa had ended, and so with it, her visa. Consequently, in a wave of creativity she identified a need and examined her unique skills to find an intersection, and thus created a business to win a visa and perpetuate her ministry among the people.

Kathy's medical background, specifically in physical therapy, along with her specialized knowledge of community health practices, gave her the skills to start a foundation working among the disabled and their families in the community of the town that borders Chantikland. The goal was to help moms figure out how to help their disabled children and more fully integrate them into the family. Through this work, Kathy would meet the necessary requirements for a visa *and* be doing great ministry among *the least of these.*

Though the ministry to the disabled was valuable, surprisingly that is not how the Lord answered this particular prayer. Rather, the three women who worked alongside Kathy in the ministry comprised both the spiritual need and the heavenly answer to this prayer.

Kathy hired Dodi as the receptionist/admin assistant for the clinic. She is a believer and the wife of a deeply respected and long-

term friend and colleague in the work among the Chantik. Then she
hired Perlu as the second physical therapist on staff and Mahu as a lay
health worker. All four women got along wonderfully.

Soon enough, the women started having substantial conversations
about their hopes, their dreams, and more than anything, their fears.
Both Perlu and Mahu were of marriageable age, and one of their
biggest concerns was about how to keep their husbands once they
had one. Among the Chantik, and within Islam, it is acceptable for
a man to divorce his wife or to marry additional wives. The fear of
either was of paramount concern to both young women.

One of the related fears was that of *infertility*. To be unable to
conceive, carry, and bear a child for one's husband is shameful in
their culture. It is the topmost reason that a man would divorce his
wife or make her the second wife, which is small consolation, at best.
When Perlu and Mahu voiced these concerns, it opened the door for
Dodi to share her story.

Dodi had been married for several years when she met these
young ladies, but had yet to conceive. The girls were aghast that her
husband hadn't divorced her in that time. Intrigued by her story, they
pressed her about what she'd done to keep him.

Their eagerness to hear Dodi's story allowed her to share, in detail,
what contributed to her being able to "keep" her husband. The first
thing she shared was that both she and her husband are Christians
who ardently believe in the Bible. She shared that barrenness is
not a legitimate reason for divorce according to the Bible, nor are
a litany of other reasons a Chantik Muslim could use as grounds
for divorce. Unfaithfulness is the sole reason given, and even that is
to be lamented if it ends in divorce. Therefore, she had confidence
that her husband would not leave her for any such reason. This
pronouncement surprised them and piqued their interest greatly.

Dodi went on to share that her confidence in her husband's

faithfulness to her was superseded only by her confidence in the Lord's *goodness*. The idea of God being *good*, as in morally excellent, made sense to the girls; but the idea of Him being good, as in *kind* and *merciful*, was beyond their understanding from their experience with Islam. Dodi shared numerous stories in the Bible where the Lord opened the womb of a barren woman to both bless her and to further His will. The Bible encourages us, as believers, to cast our cares upon Him—the Father who gives good gifts to His children.

So Dodi shared the second important part of her story. She recounted to the girls that she and her husband prayed ardently to the Lord. Every day for two years, they prayed for the Lord to open her womb. All the while they trusted in His ability to give this good gift to them, but they acknowledged that they still trusted in His plan if it wasn't His will for them to conceive.

Dodi knew that the Chantik—and people worldwide—mistakenly believe that both prayer and blessing are "a magical force or a mystical power by which someone can obtain desired benefits. In this mentality, blessing is not much more than luck or fortune that can sometimes be manipulated with procedures or by people believed to have special powers."[2]

With the tendency of locals to look at prayer like a cosmic vending machine, akin to the mentality with which they approached black magic, Dodi was careful to explain that God could still be good and not give her what she wanted. Dodi shared that the power of prayer isn't in its ability to entice God to do something that is out of His character. Rather, it gives Him yet another opportunity to reveal His character more fully by either providing what's asked for or by denying that petition in favor of His greater will to give a good gift in some other way.

Kathy watched Dodi reveal God's character in a thousand ways as she told her story. The girls hung on her every word. Though it all started as them seeking ways to keep their future husbands, it turned into one opportunity after another to sow seeds of much greater value. It is the job of every believer to pray for persons like those girls to find their value and hope in Christ alone.

· · ·

When the natural disaster hit—an event that changed so much for everyone—Kathy was on home assignment in the United States trying to figure out her next move to obtain a visa. When she learned of the destruction, she flew back and spent all ninety days of her traveler's visa trying to help the people and figure out what her place would be in the future of Chantikland.

It was therefore wholly unexpected to realize that she didn't have a place there any longer. After nearly a decade's worth of devotion to seeing Christ's church planted among the Chantik, Kathy's work among the people was at an end. True to herself, Kathy's exit from the Chantik Go Team wasn't loud or combustible. The situation simply shifted around her in such a way that it was clear the Lord was drawing her on to another path.

Other needs and other people would play the parts moving forward. But Kathy's heart for the people never ceased to beat its drum, even though she did eventually find her way home to the US. To this day, she keeps in contact with a number of her Chantik friends on Facebook and via email. Some have found the Lord, and others she still prays will find Him. In all of this, Kathy rests in the knowledge that the team gained a foothold in the province, and that though darkness reigns in much of it, the desperate need of a few was met by the saving knowledge of Christ. She still waits expectantly for the impressive harvest Christ will reap among the Chantik, and prays to that end.

LESSONS LEARNED

1. Don't assume that you have a personality that God can't use as a missionary. He made you and He calls everyone to be missional in some way.
2. The Lord rewards faithfulness.
3. Just because your first attempt doesn't meet with your idea of success doesn't mean that the Lord is done with you.
4. Never write anyone off as a lost cause. Jesus' parable in Luke 15:3-7 shows that the Lord Himself sets the example in pursuing the one lost sheep instead of staying with the ninety-nine.

Chapter 5 Citations

1. Holy Bible. New American Standard Bible. Matthew 11:28.
2. S. D. Gallagher and S. C. Hawthorne, in R. D. Winter and S. C. Hawthorne (eds.), *Perspectives on the World Christian Movement: A Reader* (4th ed., 2009). Pasadena, CA: William Carey Library.

SIX

TIM AND SANDY
LAY IT DOWN

There is an appointed time for everything. And there is a time
for every event under heaven—
A time to give birth and a time to die;
A time to plant and a time to uproot what is planted.
                              ~ Ecclesiastes 3:1-2 (NASB)

It's a thrilling experience when the Lord births in us a new dream, vision, or calling. It's the sweet spot of being in His will and filling our lungs with a deep breath of purpose. Of course, the process of accepting a new calling has challenges—it demands that we wrap our minds around the task, summon the courage, and stretch our faith to make it happen. While putting on the mantle of *calling* isn't easy, being asked to surrender that vision is often infinitely harder.

Tim and Sandy intimately know the joys of being called, living out that calling through intense challenges, and then enduring the heartache of surrendering the call when the Lord decides, in His infinite wisdom, that it is time to uproot what was planted.

Blessed In Boston

Though Tim and Sandy met in Denver, they began their married life in Boston. Up to this point, both had lived nominal Christian lives in their youth but had wandered without spiritual mentorship in their teen and college years. When Sandy joined Tim in Boston, she found a church for them to go to. Tim and Sandy both had the desire to deepen their faith, but didn't know anything beyond slipping into a pew each week before quietly slipping out. *Growing*, however, was exactly what the Lord had in mind for them at this church in Boston.

After attending for several months, the pastor *told* them, "The new members class starts at nine o'clock tomorrow morning in my office, and you need to be there." There didn't seem to be a lot of room for discussion, so the two dutifully showed up the next morning. After the membership class, they both were regularly prodded into service at the church. Serving like this was all so new and uncomfortable that they resolved to "just go and do it."

Nothing could prepare Tim and Sandy for what happened next.

Tim came home one night and announced, out of the blue, "We're moving to Pittsburgh!" He had just gotten another promotion in his company, and it required *another* transfer. Tim was thrilled, since it meant returning to his hometown. Sandy, however, was less than thrilled. Her exact words were: "This is horrible!" Sandy's hope was to come to Boston, marry Tim, and then get him to transfer back to Denver. Pittsburgh was nowhere on her agenda!

It didn't help that Sandy was several months pregnant with their first child at the time. Added to which she was having some complications, thus requiring complete bed rest for the last six weeks of her pregnancy. Not an easy thing to do while Tim was still working and they were now supposed to be moving. Nothing could prepare Tim and Sandy for what happened next.

For six full weeks church members came to the house to clean, bring meals, iron Tim's shirts, and help them pack. Since these people knew Tim and Sandy were leaving, they had no expectations that the church would get anything back from the couple by way of continued participation or additional volunteering—and that baffled Tim and Sandy.

One day, the pastor's daughter, who had led the wave of service, was ironing a shirt while Sandy looked on from the couch. Sandy asked, "Why are you doing this for us when you know that we are leaving?" The woman's response was simple: "Because one day, you'll do this for someone else."

Sandy and Tim had never witnessed, let alone personally experienced, the kind of extravagant and sacrificial love that these numerous helpers showed them week after week. It was eye-opening to receive that kind of love and care—especially when they were leaving—and consequently, it changed them forever.

Now they knew what it looked like to participate in the body of Christ in a genuine way. By their love, the church members in Boston had planted deep seeds of sacrificial love and service in Tim and Sandy's hearts. That in turn launched the couple into a season of deep spiritual growth.

A Church Homecoming

After yet another move, Tim and Sandy did return to Denver. One Sunday, they showed up at Cherry Hills Community Church for the first time. In just one Sunday, they were hooked. CHCC was a growing and enthusiastic body of believers who had the vision, energy, and depth of faith that they could learn from—a church that could be *home*.

Tim and Sandy jumped in, serving actively among the children's programs. Life seemed about as good as it could get. In addition to loving the church, they lived in a dream home, Sandy was staying home and taking care of their growing family, and Tim had the job he'd waited ten years to get. But then the Lord chose to speak to Sandy about their future. Sitting on the deck one morning, looking out across the Front Range, she heard one simple statement.

"You are going to sell everything and become a missionary."

> "You are going to sell everything and become a missionary."

Just that short and simple. Sandy knew it was a message from the Lord because that wasn't a thought she would have had on her own. She pondered what the Lord had said for days before she shared it with Tim. In fact, she waited until they were walking toward their car after a particularly good Sunday service when she said, "I think I'm being called to be a missionary."

Tim's shock was evident in his response. "Well, the Lord doesn't break up families; and I'm not called, so you need to get this out of your system."

Undeterred, Sandy called Pastor G. to share what the Lord had said to her. His assistant happened to be taking his calls that day. When Sandy stated, "I think we are being called to be missionaries," the assistant responded with a simple "Oh?" Sandy pressed forward and said, "Yes—and can you tell me what that *is*?"

After talking for an hour, the assistant pointed Sandy to the Discover the World (DTW) class, which was designed for people interested in missions. It was a step Sandy could take, and she did.

Pastor G. led the DTW class; and though Sandy went to it alone, she and Tim were in Pastor G.'s Sunday school class together. This frequent contact, and Sandy's enthusiasm, prompted ongoing conversations between the three of them about missions. Enthused by the DTW class and her growing desire to be a missionary, Sandy doggedly pursued Tim to consider the idea. Her urgency came from a good place—a desire to follow the Lord—but it fell on deaf ears with Tim.

Somewhere along the line, between the Bible study with Pastor G. and all the conversations with Sandy, the Lord began softening Tim's heart. Pastor G. challenged them to go on a short-term trip, and Tim was actually OK with the idea because he thought a trip would get it out of Sandy's system.

Years In The Making

A few months later, Tim and Sandy found themselves flying into Chantikland. The moment they landed, Sandy's heart breathed, "I'm home." She kept the thought to herself that week as she and Tim ministered, prayed, and bonded with James and Ayu, CHCC's missionary partners. At some point during the week, Tim shared how he thought they could make a real difference in Chantikland. When they were on the plane, about to leave, he said, "So, when are we coming back?" They spent the flight home next to a missionary, who just happened to be on the same flight, asking questions about how to become long-term missionaries.

To complicate things, in the weeks leading up to the trip Tim had arranged for a transfer to New Hampshire, not realizing the impact the trip would have on the course of their lives. They touched down from the trip to Chantikland and promptly moved a couple thousand miles away from CHCC—and their burgeoning conversation about going into missions long-term.

The distance and inconvenience didn't deter Pastor G. He kept in contact with Tim and Sandy regularly and dubbed them as the team leaders for the Chantik Go Team. That recognition turned out to be an ill-fated honor, since several team members were already in-country and Tim and Sandy were stuck in New Hampshire.

As months and months rolled by, Tim and Sandy grew increasingly discouraged that they would ever get to Chantikland. Their house had been on the market for months without even one prospective buyer coming to look at the property. (Winter in New Hampshire isn't prime selling season!) However, every now and then touches of encouragement and connection to their missionary calling would pop up. A prime example was when they got this phone call.

Sandy: Hello?

Church: Hi, Sandy. I'm the missions director at Indian Rocks Church in Florida, and we want to apologize for sending the video to the wrong address.

Sandy: What?

Church: Well, aren't you the team leaders for the Chantik Go Team from CHCC?

Sandy: Well . . . yes, sort of . . .

Church: Well, we sent the video to the wrong location; we didn't know that you moved!

Sandy: I'm not sure what you are talking about . . . *at all*.

Church: Well, our church is looking to adopt a people group, and we wondered if you would come down and speak at our conference in two weeks on behalf of the Chantik?

Sandy: Well . . . *Sure* . . .

Though it was impetuous, the conversation and accepted invitation all felt divine. Tim and Sandy packed up their kids and drove from New Hampshire to Florida that February to participate in the conference. When they arrived, they were informed that in the two weeks since they were invited, the church *had* chosen the Chantik as their adopted people group—and Tim and Sandy were now the featured speakers, much to their surprise! So, with 4,500 eager conference participants, they rallied to the moment. Tim and Sandy shared their heart for the Chantik, and Indian Rocks responded with their enthusiastic support.

On the drive home, Sandy turned to Tim and said, "OK, I guess this is for real, and I guess we are on our way." And though there had been no interest at all in their house, finally just one person showed up and bought it! The Lord removed that plaguing obstacle holding them back, so they packed up their three little ones and headed to Denver.

Though it took years of twists, turns, obstacles, and delays, the Lord fulfilled what He had spoken to Sandy—that she would sell everything and become a missionary. *And*, He did it all while wooing Tim to the same call. What an impressive God we serve. Time, trouble, and cost are nothing to Him. He has the big picture of His will ever in mind, and "We know that all things work together for good to those who love God, to those who are called according to *His* purpose" (Romans 8:28, NKJV).

A Hard Knock

Finally, *finally*, it was time. Tim and Sandy arrived in the home country of Chantikland, though not in the region itself. Their temporary home was in the city where the language acquisition school was located. The rest of the team was there, and several members had been studying the language for up to two years at this point.

Tim and Sandy were at a severe disadvantage. They had walked into a team that already had two years of bonding, along with an equal measure of exposure to the culture and language—and they were supposed to *lead* the team.

In the thick of trying to figure out the team dynamics, just weeks after they arrived in-country, the government experienced a coup. All of the sudden, hundreds of thousands of protesters were out in the streets of the capital of the country. In their own slightly smaller city, huge and violent rallies were happening daily. The situation was definitely unstable, prompting regular phone calls from the Venture Group to ensure that the team had an evacuation plan.

The team felt conflicted; those who had been there for a while felt safe enough to stay, as long as they were cautious, but Sandy understandably feared for her children. Tim decided that he would stay with the team but get Sandy and the kids to a nearby country until the heat of the protests died down. It wasn't a great solution, but it was the only one they could come up with. Sensing Sandy's hesitation, Gwen volunteered to go with her and the kids out of the country.

The airport, in response to the rapidly increasing demand to leave the area, pulled out every plane that was even remotely capable of flight. Sandy and Gwen got on their plane with the kids, who were one, three, and six years old at the time, and listened to the plane try to start its ancient engine again and again. *Blummm, blum, blum, blum. Blummm, blum, blum, blum.*

The longer the plane failed to spring to life, the more the panic rose in Sandy. Eyes wide, she looked at Gwen, who calmly replied, "Don't worry, it's not my day to die."

Taking Leaps

A couple weeks later, Tim joined his family to assure them that it was safe to return and that he had a vision for their next steps. They flew back to their temporary base and almost as quickly hopped on a flight to Chantikland to visit James and Ayu. These faithful missionary partners, with whom Tim and Sandy had bonded on their first trip and in the years between, welcomed their arrival. By the end of that short trip, the momentum of their determination and enthusiasm propelled them to action. Wheels were in motion for visas to be arranged through English Around the World for Tim, Sandy, and the kids and any other Chantik Go Team member who wanted to come.

Tim and Sandy rejoined the team and communicated the urgency they felt to get into the region. These visas were their shot, and they were going to take it. They extended the opportunity to "enter the land" to the whole Go Team. It was a polarizing offer for sure. The coup in the main part of the country had subsided, but the civil war in Chantikland was raging and the dynamics in the team were equally unstable. Tim and Sandy were effectively like Joshua and Caleb, who had seen the land they were called to and who had come back with a fire in them to persuade the others that it was time for the Go Team to enter Chantikland. It was a *now-or-never* moment, more than they could have ever known at the time.

The visas took a couple months to arrange, and during that time the whole team sought the Lord in prayer. Eventually, Kathy decided to go with Tim and Sandy to be an English teacher through the EAW program. Gwen also went with them, but she had her own visa through another organization related to her work with importing and exporting businesses. The remaining two members of the team *did not* enter Chantikland. They felt called to leave the Chantik Go Team and partner with another Venture Group team, whose focus was on a different people group.

• • •

After a half-dozen years of CHCC praying, preparing, sending, and supporting the Chantik Go Team, the four remaining members entered the land as Christ's ambassadors. They worked alongside of James and Ayu, CHCC's long-term missionary partners and friends, in a dynamic season of opportunity. The Lord's plan is always to win to Himself people from every nation, tribe, and language (Revelation 7:9); and His preferred method is to use flawed men and women to accomplish this task. In doing so, He demonstrates to the world that it is by His strength that all things are possible.

All of this history—the *difficulties, relational dynamics,* and *differing calls*—was not outside of God's redemptive plan. The season in Chantikland would turn out to be relatively short-lived for the Go Team because of the civil war. They were granted visas for a total of about two and a half years before being kicked out, resulting in their working outside the region and switching their focus to training and sending nationals in. That short span, in and of itself, makes sense of the urgency felt to enter the land. The Lord propelled them to action—and thank God He did!

TALKING THE TALK

PRAYER #3: *"Pray for Christians to be willing to step through the open door for English language teachers to the Chantik."*

The visas provided through English Around the World were an extraordinary gift to Tim and Sandy. The program had already been operating for several years by the time they came on board, establishing it as a well-respected entity whose English teachers were highly sought after. EAW's program employed a trickle-down philosophy of education by having teachers—like Tim—train the local high school English teachers in conversational English.

Tim was assigned to the most prestigious high school in the capital of Chantikland, the same school where Kathy (chapter 5) was also assigned. This school was so favored by the elite that it had the reputation that it would produce the next president of Chantikland.

Because of the high expectations for the school, the program encouraged frequent interaction between Tim and his students (the teachers) to encourage rapid linguistic improvement. This meant he got to see the same teachers multiple times a week, for months on end, both in the classroom and in social settings. The frequent interaction jump-started Tim and Sandy's community involvement and fostered genuine kinship between their family and several key students, Eccarikkai and Chomnuoy. The relationships between these two men and Tim (and eventually Sandy) lasted for years, well beyond the time when they lived in close proximity in Chantikland.

THE LAY OF THE LAND

PRAYER #36: *"Pray for the men who will one day be leaders among the Chantik. May they hear and respond to the gospel at the proper time in their lives."*

Initially, all the interactions between Tim and Eccarikkai were in class as one English teacher to another. It wasn't long, however, before the men realized how much they enjoyed each other's company. This led to one-on-one time outside of class. As their friendship grew, Eccarikkai offered to teach Tim about Chantikland by driving him to various areas in and around the capital and telling him stories as they went.

One day, as the two men drove along a beach, Eccarikkai stopped and said, "Look, you *know* that we don't allow missionaries here." Eccarikkai turned and pointed. "You see this beach? The first missionaries tried to land here three hundred years ago, but we cut their heads off in the water, so that they didn't ever reach our soil. And I'm telling you that if a missionary comes again, we'd do the same today."

The statement hung in the air between them, crackling with tension. In the moment, fear bubbled out of Tim in the form of gales of laughter. Surprisingly, Tim's reaction broke the tension between them, and Eccarikkai didn't press the issue any further by asking Tim outright if he was a missionary. Instead, they just started driving again and the conversation went on in other directions.

Eccarikkai, a genuine friend to Tim, was not ready to hear the Good News of the gospel. However, maybe one day he *will* have ears to hear, and *that* is what we need to pray for—both among the Chantik and all the unreached peoples of the world.

THE BLIND EYE OF A FRIEND

PRAYER #35: *"Ask for God's choice of future leaders to be put in place, whose lives can serve to advance His Kingdom."*

Ripe for relationship making, Tim met Chomnuoy (whose nickname was Noy) as another one of his English students through the EAW classes. At the time, Noy was still just a regular English teacher in the high school, but he was ambitious and highly intelligent. Constantly eager to improve his conversational English, Noy befriended Tim initially for that purpose, though he was already quite fluent.

Noy and his wife soon began to spend a considerable amount of time with Tim and Sandy. They each had children, and the simple act of sharing a meal brought joy to both families. It wasn't uncommon for the families to get together for special occasions; so, of course, they celebrated Noy's promotion to a position of influence under the Education and Culture Minister in the Chantik government.

On one hand, Noy's promotion made him a danger to Tim and Sandy because of how high up in the government he arose. But the relationship they'd built with him and his family was so strong that they chose to see it as a *blessing* despite the potential danger. Noy must have been of a similar opinion, because while he was very well educated and had learned about missionaries through years spent in the West, he never directly asked, which meant they never had to directly admit to being missionaries. There was every possibility that he knew what Tim and Sandy were about, but he valued the relationship like they did, so he chose to turn a blind eye to their true purpose for being in Chantikland.

Though Noy has yet to find Christ as Lord and Savior, he is still a good friend approaching two decades later. Who knows how God might use this man of influence, this man who has shown favor and friendship to believers for all these years? The story of King Nebuchadnezzar showing favor to Daniel comes to mind.

While we don't know if or how the Lord will use Noy to advance His Kingdom, we do know that additional seeds of love and relationship are planted with emails, with authentic friendship, and every time Tim and Sandy return to Chantikland. We know this because it is their faithful friend Noy who acts as their host, welcoming them back each time.

POOR IN SPIRIT AND SHORT ON SUPPLIES

PRAYER #58: *"Pray that God would raise up Christians who would be willing to serve and reach out to the Chantik poor."*

As soon as they moved to Chantikland, Tim and Sandy hit the ground running. Tim was teaching English classes at the high school and Sandy was homeschooling the three kids. Both were working with teammates Kathy and Gwen, as well as longtime ministry partners and friends, James and Ayu. One of the projects that consumed a good amount of time and energy was outreach to those affected by the civil war.

For the most part, the active fighting between the rebels and the national military happened out in the hills and mountains outside of the capital city, where Tim and Sandy lived. There were enough days, however, that tensions in town would rise to a fever pitch with protests or news of some new atrocity committed by one side or the other. Whole villages were being caught in the middle of violent clashes, and the villagers, fearing for their lives, would flee into the nearest mosque for safety. The problem was that they were so afraid of the war around them that they weren't coming out—even for food. And, they were beginning to starve.

1 CARGO CONTAINER OF FOOD STUFFS & MEDICAL SUPPLIES FOR REFUGEES

During the early months of being in Chantikland, Sandy had become the warden of the US embassy—a role that had some perks. As warden, Sandy kept track of the whopping twelve Westerners who lived in the region and passed on any alerts or critical information the embassy wanted disseminated. While the "job" was small, the connections weren't. It meant that she knew the right ears to bend to ask for humanitarian aid to support the outreach they wanted to do for those trapped in mosques up in the hills.

Sandy called home, and through contacts made by Beth (the home-based team advocate) she was able to coordinate with Samaritan's Purse to acquire a full shipping container of rice and beans. For weeks on end, they'd load up James and Ayu's van with their chickens, the rice and beans, and personal hygiene items donated from supporting churches. They would stuff it full to the gills and send it to the latest locations under attack. However, *send* isn't the right word. Ayu, a physically small, yet lionhearted woman, personally drove it up into the warzone.

Ayu was the only non-Western team member and the only national of Chantikland, which gave her more freedom to travel than the rest of the Go Team. So she, with just two locals to assist her, would travel from mosque to mosque, delivering vanloads of food and supplies. Each time, she'd say: "You may not want it, but this food is given to you in the name of Jesus." The people were so desperate that they gratefully accepted the food from Jesus.

[Read the full story about delivering the food and supplies in "An Angel on the Road" in chapter 3.]

A HELPFUL HANDYMAN

PRAYER #22: *"Praise God for the friendships in the capital city that cross ethnic lines. Pray for this favor to continue so that God might bless the 'nations' through the Chantik."*

During all the eventfulness of supporting the food and supply runs to the mosques, Tim and Sandy still had to deal with the normal tasks of life—shopping, cooking, teaching school, and home maintenance. They lived in a nice enough home in the capital, but as with all homes, periodically things needed fixing—things best left to a professional. That's when Sudi, the handyman, entered their story.

Sudi had come as a recommendation from a Chantik friend, and Tim and Sandy liked him immediately. He got to work on their list of projects, and over time he turned from a reliable worker into a real friend. The Chantik are wonderfully friendly, though not quick to trust. Knowing that made Sudi's genuine affection for the family all the sweeter as their friendship grew.

As the couple got to know Sudi better, they learned he was originally from a village in the middle of the civil unrest. In fact, his village was known for being the home of the rebels. Once, Tim jokingly asked, "Are you a rebel?" and Sudi smilingly avoided answering the question. Since there were questions that Tim and Sandy didn't want to answer outright either, they let it go.

What they started to notice, however, was that Sudi would take pains to take care of them. He would come to their house on certain days and warn them to stay inside or stay close to home. Sure enough, soon thereafter they would hear of some violence they had avoided by heeding his advice. As much as he could, Sudi protected Tim and Sandy's family from the war around them.

A TRUE BEGINNING

PRAYER #13: *"Pray for many Muslims to honestly face the questions they have about Islam (e.g., Why after fasting for the month of Ramadan can you still have evil or hateful thoughts about others if the fasting was supposed to purify your heart?). Pray they would find the answer to these questions in Jesus' cleansing blood."*

The typical house in Chantikland was built with windows that run practically from floor to ceiling—and without screens. This unusual design feature was the means by which the Lord brought another amazing group of people into Sandy and Tim's lives. These enormous windows are wonderful for circulating the breeze, but a nightmare when it comes to keeping the feral cats out of the kitchen!

The job of building screens for the unique windows was beyond the talents of Sudi, so Tim and Sandy received a recommendation for a highly talented family of carpenters and seamstresses, whom we'll call the Woods family. The father, Chatot, valued education highly; and through his labors he provided for all of his children to go to college (even the girls). However, he also thought it was prudent for his children to have a practical trade if they fell on hard times. Thus his sons learned carpentry at his side and his daughters learned to be superior seamstresses from his wife, Kaati.

Building the screens was a big project, and different family members rotated through the job as they were available. This regular and varied interaction allowed Tim and Sandy, and even Kathy and Gwen, to meet the whole family over time. Friendship blossomed between the family and Go Team members.

Friendship led to familiarity, and the Woods family felt free to express their curiosity about the Go Team members. On one occasion Sandy had left a Bible atlas laying out after a homeschooling lesson for the kids. Seeing it, Abang (one of the sons) asked if it was a Bible. Sandy explained that it was a book with maps of places and events in the Bible, but that the Bible was a separate book.

Several weeks later, Abang brought one of his sisters, Filza, to the house and had her knock on the door and ask for a Bible. Sandy was immediately on alert. While they had been developing a wonderful friendship, it was illegal to give a Bible to a Muslim, so she wasn't quite sure how to respond. Sandy ushered Filza and Abang into the house and asked them if their father knew what they were asking. Filza explained that Chatot had actually sent her to ask for a Bible.

The month of Ramadan (the Islamic holy month of fasting) was upon them, and Chatot had learned that Christians also fast. He wanted his family to read the Bible and study why Christians would fast in comparison to why Muslims do so. Completely aghast, Sandy marveled at this unbelievable (and scary) request. She sent Filza and Abang home empty-handed that day, but with a promise that she'd look for a Bible they could keep.

In a team meeting, Tim, Sandy, Gwen, and Kathy all agreed that the Woods family had shown enough genuine curiosity that they didn't feel this was a trap. The Woods family wanted a Bible, and the team was going to make that happen. The solution of how to do so safely (or safer) became clear with Gwen's burgeoning plans to move out of the region to a trade hub just outside of Chantikland. Gwen could give them a Bible right before her departure and be safely out of the region should there be any backlash.

Soon enough, the Woods family came for a visit and left with a copy of the Bible in one of the national languages they could read easily. God's Word doesn't return void, and it certainly didn't in the case of the Woods family.

FROM ONE FATHER TO ANOTHER

PRAYER #40: *"Pray for fathers' relationships with their families. These men could be a light to their community and extended family in the way they love their families. Ask God to work a radical transformation in their hearts."*

Fathers in Chantikland fight a genuine sense of disconnectedness with their children. Men are typically sent out to other districts to look for work and only return home when they have money to share. Chatot struggled against this issue. His carpentry business allowed him to stay relatively close to home, with enough projects to keep him busy, but it was his philosophy of education that gave him a vision for how to connect with his children. He valued both formal education and learning a trade. Consequently, he intentionally spent significant amounts of time with his children teaching and training them.

Though he was an avid reader, Chatot gleaned just as much from the world around him as he did from books. Chatot diligently endeavored to be a good father, and he was, but one day he was mesmerized as he watched Tim play with his children. Tim wasn't doing anything mind-blowing or unusual (in his opinion); he was simply tickling his kids and chasing them around the room, delighting in their squeals and laughter. For whatever reason, this was a completely new experience of fathering for Chatot, and he later shared that it influenced the man he wanted to be.

Often, the best witness is simply to live what you believe in front of others, who are most certainly watching you.

A MAN OF PEACE

PRAYER #39: *"Pray for Chantik fathers—that God would prepare their hearts to receive the gospel. Pray that they would have courage to embrace Christ and that their families would follow."*

The screen-building project lasted only for a time, but the relationship between families lasted much longer. The children would spend time in each other's homes, and the families would invite each other over for dinner. The first time that Tim and Sandy went for a visit at the Woods' home, Tim and Chatot got into a deep conversation about Abraham Lincoln. Chatot had found a book about the former president of the United States, and the man impressed him greatly.

Tim's curiosity at Chatot's willingness to read about an American president was only surpassed by his surprise at Chatot's impression of the president's life. Chatot explained that he greatly respected President Lincoln as a "man of peace." Chatot acknowledged the wars fought, but the fact that Lincoln would fight to free people from a different ethnic group represented an incredibly honorable life. That

Lincoln would ultimately give his life for that cause, or as a result of it, caused Chatot to see this man's legacy as one worthy of high praise.

Chatot's view of President Lincoln's life, struggle, and victory over slavery was beautiful. That he could value these virtues in a person so different than himself made it easier to talk to Chatot about another man who lived a sacrificial life. A man who lived, and died, to bring freedom to those who were slaves under unrelenting masters: Sin and Death. Only the mysterious ways of God could account for a president of the United States, 150 years in his grave, prompting a conversation about Jesus.

While we'll never know if Chatot gave his life to Christ, due to his premature death, we do know that his curiosity about Jesus was profound. We can celebrate that one of his daughters and his wife came to faith in Christ, and they remain in contact with several of the Go Team members to this day. It seems that Chatot became what he admired so much, a man of peace, allowing Jesus to enter his family.

•   •   •

In the end, Sandy and Tim were in Chantikland for about eighteen months. That seems like a short time, and yet eighteen months was plenty of time for the Lord to accomplish His will through these two dedicated servants. Leaving wasn't easy for them. Their hearts longed to stay, but the Lord changed their path, requiring them to head home to deal with some medical concerns, which ultimately prevented their return.

Surrender is a painful process, one that can and did last for years. Living and working among the Chantik was the fulfillment of a calling that took ten years to build up to and more than that to fully surrender. But the Lord is good. His mercies are new every morning. Tim and Sandy have visited from time to time and still keep in contact with a number of their Chantik friends.

Their "take away" from following the Lord to Chantikland and back again is this: "When you are truly in the center of God's will, there is a confidence that comes with being there. You know that whether you live or die, God is in control. That knowledge brings real peace. And, Sandy said it best when she shared, "People shouldn't think there is some reservoir of clean, shiny, *super* Christians whom God is going to use for missions. He uses ordinary people to do extraordinary things."

LESSONS LEARNED

1. The Lord can use any willing person to do His will.
2. Be patient and know that the Lord is at work in your life, even if it takes years of incremental steps to see where you're headed.
3. The Lord can work redemptively in every situation.
4. Surrender is a critical means by which the Lord can encourage you to grow in your faith.

SEVEN

BOB AND BECCA SHAKE IT UP

No one pours new wine into old wineskins. Otherwise, the wine will burst the skins, and both the wine and the wineskins will be ruined. No, they pour new wine into new wineskins.

~Mark 2:22 (NIV)

By the time Bob and Becca reached the field, it had been five years since the first Go Team members had been there and three years since most of them had left. The region was closed. The civil war was raging. Visas were all but impossible to get.

If they had come to do what had been done before, it wouldn't have worked. Chantikland was different. Gwen and Kathy, the remaining team members, were different. And, more than anything, Bob and Becca were different. Trying to put these two new, enthusiastic leaders into the old vision would have been putting new wine into old wineskins. But, of course, that isn't where their story *started*.

Called To The Kingdom

It is a beautiful thing when any person gets saved, but it is particularly beautiful when an adult does—one who has seen the world without the hope of Christ and doesn't want to live like that anymore. It's even better when two of them make that choice, together.

. . .

Bob and Becca were already deep into their careers and family life when the Lord plucked their heartstrings and called them to Himself. It started with Becca accepting an invitation from a tenacious friend to attend a Precepts Bible study class with her. At that point in Becca's life, she and Bob had been attending what was functionally a Unitarian church, but it didn't preach Christ as Savior, nor preach about Him at all.

Bob and Becca were already deep into their careers and family life when the Lord plucked their heartstrings and called them to Himself.

It was in the Precepts class with her friend that Becca came to accept Jesus as her Lord and Savior. She didn't, however, tell Bob about her decision at that time. It turns out, she didn't need to; the Lord was about to make His own introductions to Bob.

Around the time of the Precepts class—and Becca's decision to follow Christ—Bob was invited to a Promise Keeper's event by a friend of his who attended Cherry Hills Community Church. It was there, at the event, that Bob, as he puts it, "met the Holy Spirit—and it terrified me." Bob goes on to recount that he "had seen and heard the true God and didn't know what to do about it." As the two men discussed Bob's reaction, the friend suggested that he figure out who Jesus is first, and then decide how to proceed.

This same friend followed up that suggestion with an invitation to a Wednesday night Bible study at CHCC. It was in that Bible study that Bob made a decision for Christ and Becca revealed her decision. For Bob and Becca, accepting Christ was just the first step in what has turned out to be a very active pursuit of Him ever since.

What We'll Do For Our Children

Fast-forward a handful of years—Becca is on staff at Cherry Hills in children's ministry and Bob is quite active in the church as well. And their eleven-year-old daughter "just happens" to pick up a book that would change all of their lives. A biography of Mother Teresa inspired their daughter profoundly. All she wanted to do from that point on was to become a nurse and be a missionary.

Like many parents before them, and many to come, Bob and Becca wanted to be supportive of their little girl's dream. The problem was that they didn't know much about what a missionary did or what that life would look like. To address that gap in their understanding, they took the missions class at CHCC. There seeds of thought were planted that would ultimately lead *them* to the mission field, *not* their daughter—though she did eventually become a nurse.

It seems the Lord always knows how to use just the right messenger to start a conversation of thought in our heads and hearts, our children being chief among the most influential.

A Season Of Change

Around the same window of time that they took the missions class, Becca was asked to participate in the children's side of an in-country retreat for the Go Team missionaries in Chantikland. Pastor G. also invited Bob to come on the trip. Unfortunately, the political instability didn't allow the retreat to be held in Chantikland, so it took place instead in a resort city not far from the region. Here Bob and Becca reunited with Gwen and Kathy, as well as a few other team members. Bob and Becca had met all of the team before, but this was a focused time to connect.

Just after that trip, Bob was invited to join the men's ministry at CHCC, and everything seemed to be sailing along for a contented couple in ministry in the suburbs. But the Lord wasn't done. He had more for them. He inspired them to take a second trip the following summer.

On that trip the Lord started prompting their hearts for the lost in that region specifically. In Chantikland the Muslim call to prayer goes out over loudspeakers in some areas and the radio station in others. The first call is in the predawn hour, and each day on that trip the first call would ring out and wake up the whole team. Typically, they could all get back to sleep; but the Lord chose that time to speak to Becca. He pressed on her heart to pray to Him on behalf of the millions around her who were praying to Allah.

The Lord used that early morning prayer time to plant another seed in her heart—one that wouldn't be satisfied with short-term trips (as valuable as they can be). That prayer time definitively changed things for Becca. At the same time, Bob was being moved in other ways on the trip. He couldn't stop thinking about the pressing need of the Chantik. Together, they left with long-term thoughts on their minds. However, all seeds need time to grow.

Shortly after that second trip, the Chantik Go Team began to unravel. Several members of the team left the Chantik-focused team to join the Venture Group's regional team, and just a year and half after that Tim and Sandy, the Go Team leaders, had to come home for health reasons. That left just Gwen and Kathy in the field, in two different cities, and James and Ayu were in yet a third city.

After a time, Pastor G. asked Bob and Becca to return to Chantikland with him to pray and assess the situation. They went with their minds open to new directions and ready to respond to the situation in the field as it *was,* and not just trying to press on with the original mandate of the Go Team. So much had changed, the vision and direction of the team needed to change with it.

This trip resulted in a wonderful collaboration between Pastor G., Bob, Becca, Gwen, and Kathy. They agreed that the time when Western missionaries were the frontline workers in Chantikland had passed, at least for this season of the ministry. Instead, they saw that working with, aiding, and empowering nationals and regional individuals (who could still gain entry into Chantikland) would be the key to the next wave of ministry among the Chantik.

Though the rough patch of the first team's dissolution was discouraging for everyone, the Lord redeemed it with another occasion to say, "We are hard pressed on every side, but not crushed; perplexed, but not in despair; persecuted, but not abandoned; struck down, but not destroyed."[1] He took what was broken and rebuilt it under a new banner with a new direction.

It was on this third trip, while discussing the new direction, that Pastor G. challenged Bob and Becca to consider leaving the Home Team to join the Go Team as the new team leaders. This challenge was water to the seed planted over a year before on that second trip. To honor the challenge they took steps to seek guidance from CHCC leadership, staff, and friends.

After months of prayer, and a long road to commissioning, Bob and Becca committed themselves to become the team leaders of the next wave of CHCC's effort among the Chantik. Their commitment spurred a new wave of enthusiasm, as the Home Team swelled to over forty members who prayed diligently for the mission among the Chantik. Ultimately, it was less than five years from the time Bob and Becca learned what a missionary was to when they relocated as full-time workers themselves.

The Set Up

Bob and Becca arrived on the field and went straight into language school for a year. Gwen, Bob, and Becca were all living in the same city at that time, which allowed for coordinated thought and planning of next steps. They saw themselves back up in the border town close to Chantikland, where Gwen had lived and Kathy was still living. Getting into Chantikland wasn't an option at that moment, with the civil war raging, but there were so many Chantik people who had left the region and settled in and near the border town that opportunities abounded to minister there.

As language school came to a close, their visas would expire as well. Bob had to find legitimate work to do to get a visa. The challenge was that it had to be work that would also facilitate the ministry of equipping local Christians, which was the new direction for the team. Fortunately, the Lord goes before us and behind us. God opened the door to a long-term visa through one of Gwen's connections.

Gwen had a friend, Kuo-sinn, who was a Christian businessman of local/regional decent who grew up in Chantikland. He had a heart for the work they were doing to minister to the Chantik and was interested in helping. Kuo-sinn lived in the capital city and was the owner of a large, successful consulting firm. He was already in the process of expanding his consulting firm when Gwen introduced him to Bob.

The opportunity, the need, and the solution for both Kuo-sinn and Bob became apparent. Though Kuo-sinn had a couple different cities in mind to open a new branch, meeting Bob made the decision. The first branch would be in the border town of Chantikland, and Bob would hire and mentor the branch manager and staff. This got Bob and Becca long-term visas and positioned them perfectly for what the future held.

TESTING, TESTING, 1, 2, 3 . . .

PRAYER #51: *"As the Chantik people desire to emulate the West, pray they only emulate what is helpful for a developing country and reject that which is ungodly."*

PRAYER #2: *"Pray for media to contain more Christian values for the Chantik. Ask for their discernment to filter out sensational and immoral programming."*

In the initial year of setting up the consulting business in the border town, Bob enjoyed the unusual opportunity of hosting a weekly radio program on the local station. On the show, he taught about corporate performance and personnel development. Sharing healthy concepts of work, as told through the lens of a Christian businessman, was surprisingly well received by locals. Bob's radio program had quite a following.

Rather than encouraging the corporate greed and irresponsibility that can plague businesses worldwide, Bob advocated practices and principles that fall in line with Ephesians 4:29 (NIV):

> *Do not let any unwholesome talk come out of your mouths, but only what is helpful for building others up according to their needs, that it may benefit those who listen.*

And it did benefit them. Bob's show gave locals an opportunity to expand their knowledge and improve how they did business. It also helped the consulting branch build networks throughout the city.

A NEW DIRECTION

PRAYER #28: *"Pray for favor and acceptance for Christian workers in these tightly knit, same-thinking communities."*

The consulting business was gaining traction through various branding efforts, and Bob and Becca were building trust with the leadership of the local training school for church planters. The school, which Gwen had started several years earlier, was currently being run by locals with heavy involvement from Kathy.

Then, everything changed in an instant. The natural disaster hit Chantikland like a sledgehammer. For years to come, the people and the land would suffer in the wake of its impact. The whole course of Bob and Becca's ministry changed as a result. It had to. The storm produced unspeakable need in an instant.

Innumerable conversations, decisions, and actions took place in the first days after the disaster. Bob pulled together the handful of Venture Group workers in the area to discuss needs and next steps. Among them were Gwen and a man named Danny. (Kathy had left just a couple weeks before for a home assignment.)

This group became the Venture Group's "forward" team. Their border town had an international airport and was as close as you could get without actually being in the disaster zone. Groups from around the hemisphere were making contact through organizational channels and offering help.

Within days the group found a way to send Danny on a survey trip. Arriving in the capital city of Chantikland, he saw devastation everywhere he looked. He prayerfully chose a direction and went from village to village assessing the need. In each village, Danny talked to any community leaders he could find. He was a man of peace bringing the good news that help was coming. His respectful and sensitive approach helped build a foundation of trust that the team would later build on.

Danny came back to "home base" and shared with the group what he saw, what was needed, and where he thought they should start. This was the birth of "Salem Chantik"—a project formed to respond to the disaster.

Within two weeks the other members of the home base group were able to enter the affected area and bring much-needed food and medical supplies. The groundwork that Danny had laid in talking with village leaders in one particular area, roughly a ten-kilometer stretch of coastline, opened the door to help six villages there.

How Do You Eat An Elephant?
One Bite At A Time.

While the initial efforts of the Salem Chantik project were focused entirely on medical relief and partnership with international emergency aid organizations, the whole of the project was a well-conceived response to a mass of would-be long-term problems. In partnership with World Relief, Salem Chantik developed a four-pronged approach, addressing the major issues of *health care, housing, economic development,* and *local governance capacity building.*

Bob and Becca's home in the border town quickly became insufficient as a base of operations due to the sheer volume of people coming through. They jumped on renting a building in town to act as the staging area, training facility, and launching pad for the numerous teams coming through. This became known as the resource center. Then, they rented two buildings in the capital of Chantikland as an on-site base of operations for the execution of the four-pronged plan.

LET THE LITTLE CHILDREN COME

PRAYER #4: *"Pray for the basic needs of the Chantik to be met: health care, dental care, sanitation."*

The needs related to the first prong of Salem Chantik—*health care*—were massive. The team assumed that emergency needs such as wounds and broken bones caused by the disaster would be the focus, but instead they discovered that their target area had the beautiful, unrelenting, and overwhelming need for a birthing center. Babies were going to come no matter how inopportune the timing.

Salem Chantik immediately turned the second building they had rented into a birthing center. Because scores of midwives had been lost in the disaster, the facility also became a training ground for midwives through a partnership with Johns Hopkins University, which brought in educators month after month to train those

1 BIRTHING CENTER BUILT

willing to learn midwifery. This multi-organizational partnership helped the people in the short-term and addressed the long-term need for basic reproductive medical care in those communities. It represented a wonderful collaboration between aid agencies and the local health department.

The Salem Chantik birthing center brought dozens of babies into the world, including several sets of twins. And, with all that opportunity to learn, midwives were fully trained and able to actively work throughout the district.

CONSTRUCTING THE FUTURE

PRAYER #27: *"Pray for community-building traditions, which are not strictly Islamic, to gain popularity."*

The second prong and pressing need addressed by Salem Chantik was the need for *housing*. Some areas in these six villages were wiped clean of their houses, businesses, and even their trees. Other areas had huge mounds of debris. In both instances houses were lost or badly damaged. In addition to the challenge of distributing materials and organizing and training the labor, the team was forced to address the tricky question of whose house you build first.

These tightly knit communities came together in town-hall style meetings—sometimes several hundred people at a time—and Bob and Danny would say, "We are here with a group of organizations that want to help." Then, the leaders of the community would essentially ask themselves, "What do we want to do, and do we want to work with these guys?"

Danny and Bob were excellent at building buy-in from the community, and that helped the leaders move forward when they were still in shock at the devastating losses of life and livelihood. The community meetings produced decisions regarding the two big issues: 1) What would the design of the house be? and 2) Who got the first house, and the second, and the third, etc.?

Bob turned to Gwen for her connections. He needed community organizers, carpenters, and an architect—and he needed them quickly. Reaching out to her network of like-minded organizations and agencies across the country, Gwen was able to pull together a handful of competent, faithful individuals who could function as community organizers for these massive projects.

While Gwen was rustling up community organizers, Bob and

Danny focused on getting the plans for the houses designed. They drew a rough sketch of a house to approach the village leaders with. They needed a sense of what the locals were looking for in the new construction. That simple sketch was just the beginning. The Lord blessed this effort by prompting a friend of Bob's—a Christian architect who lived in the border town—to donate his services and draw up multiple iterations of the house plans. The last iteration received high praise from the local leaders, as one bellowed, "*That* is a Chantik house!"

This massive effort spanned all six villages, with the community organizers coordinating communication between the many moving pieces. Each house had its own construction team—led by the homeowner—and Salem Chantik provided the technical supervision. World Relief sourced the materials and Salem Chantik managed the field warehouse and logistics of distribution. In all of this, the community organizers became vital parts of the community. Several of those initial organizers are still in those communities, a decade or so later, and still with the heart of church planters and disciple makers.

In the two years following the disaster, Salem Chantik built 361 new homes and repaired 176 homes. That meant that these ambassadors for Christ helped meet 537 families' basic need for shelter. Though some of the villagers had lost everything, they now had a place to start over.

THIS IS THE DAY . . . FOR SHOE DAY!

PRAYER #15: *"For young children, ask the Lord to give them experiences of love and generosity not steeped in Islamic practice."*

The people in one of the villages had a peculiar problem, which was brought to the attention of the Salem Chantik staff by their community organizer, Rahib. The children in this village were unable to go to school because they had no shoes. Whether their shoes had been lost in the disaster, swept away with the debris, or become outgrown—these children simply needed shoes.

Becca heard this request and hatched a plan. There were a number of wholesalers near the resource center back in the border town, and she would find one that would create the simple black shoes required for schools in Chantikland. But she had to have an idea of sizes and quantities. Rahib went throughout the village, collecting the sizes required for each family in the village. As quickly as he could, the cobbler then created shoes in the vast quantities that Becca needed.

Finally, the day arrived to deliver the shoes. Becca and two Salem Chantik teammates drove to the center of the village to the open-air community center, effectively a roof on pillars with no walls. They piled dozens upon dozens of shoes by size and stood back and waited. Word travels fast in a village, so swarms of children were soon searching the piles. Parents started showing up with little ones in tow and helping in the search.

Before long, word had spread to a nearby village, and one dad showed up on a motorcycle with three of his children! All in all, well over 150 pairs of shoes were given to the school-age children of that village, along with some of their neighbors.

ONE HAND WASHES THE OTHER

PRAYER #1A: *"Pray for the [Chantik] government—continued openness to American business and American people."*

Because the natural disaster was so pervasive, with waves of its destructive force unleashing an indescribable magnitude, it simply devoured everything in its path. It swallowed harbors, businesses, homes, and boats en masse. The numerous villages affected were largely agricultural and fishing communities. This devastated a major portion of the economy, resulting in the third prong of the Salem Chantik project: *economic development.*

Among the six villages, two boat works (i.e., businesses that build boats) were constructed. Each one not only hired their staff from the community, putting men to work, but the newly constructed boats also allowed fishermen once again to feed their families and the community at large. This was a critical piece of the overall recovery, since the food supply had been badly damaged. The storm had distributed debris, rubbish, and refuse across countless square miles of formerly thriving crops. The produce was lost for at least the next growing season.

Many of the fishermen were back to work, but another need arose that spurred the creation of a complementary business. It became apparent that an ice supplier was needed. Access to ice allowed the fishermen to get their catch to market and to keep the fish fresh longer. Salem Chantik found a strategic location among the villages and erected a building that would house a large freezer. Its construction put men to work, and its distribution of ice helped spur the fishermen's business by preserving the quality of their fish. Every entrepreneurial idea Salem Chantik attempted met a direct need, hired more people, and solved two problems with one stroke.

In addition to building the boat works and the ice factory and reconstructing businesses that had been in the villages, Salem Chantik moved into the next phase of their economic development strategy: providing microgrants and other forms of gifts-in-kind to prime the economic pump of village families. To those whose livelihood was on the sea, they supplied a boat or fishing nets; farmers received tools, seed, fertilizer, and equipment; herders and livestock raisers were given a calf or two young goats. Whatever the form, the beginnings of business were seeded in those families for them to make of it what they could. Getting families back to work helped everyone.

THE UNOFFICIAL REQUEST

PRAYER #34: *"Pray that Christians who go among the Chantik could find favor in the eyes of local leaders."*

Just like Danny had gone to the village leaders to lay the initial groundwork of Salem Chantik, Bob did the same with the local bureaucracy—which bloomed into the fourth prong of *local governance capacity building.* At the bureau Bob met Kamnan, the local official who inherited the task of managing the nongovernmental organizations (NGOs) wanting to work with the villages in his district. The district had roughly twelve thousand residents; and yet, when the disaster made world news, it wasn't long before Kamnan had seventy-five international aid organizations clamoring to help his people.

Kamnan's normally low-pressure job managing the needs of his constituents turned into a circus. Thankfully, Bob, on behalf of Salem Chantik, was among the first organizational representatives to offer help, and the two men really hit it off. Bob worked with Kamnan closely, and a real sense of trust and friendship was built.

At one point, when Kamnan was so overwhelmed with the pushiness of the NGOs and dealing with his own grief at having lost family members and only barely having survived the disaster himself, he turned to Bob with a plea. "Can you just take over and do the job of dealing with the NGOs?"

Prayerfully, and firmly, Bob responded, "No. But I can help you do the job *yourself.*"

For the next two years, Salem Chantik served Kamnan by mapping the district, indexing which NGOs were doing what and where, and facilitating a biweekly forum with NGO reps. Bob walked alongside Kamnan, mentoring him by helping him prepare decisions and manage the desires and needs of the local village leaders. It would have been easy for Bob to say yes to Kamnan's plea to control all those resources, but Bob chose wisely when he decided instead to invest in the man.

Since the Chantik do not trust easily, it is almost incomprehensible that a Chantik man would be willing to give over control of anything—especially to a *foreigner*. Therefore, the favorable view that Kamnan had of Bob, and the trust and respect that marked their friendship, was evidence of the fact that the Lord was working in their relationship.

TAKE IT WHILE IT'S HOT

PRAYER #1: *"Pray for the [Chantik] government—continued openness to American business and American people . . ."*

After the disaster, there was a season of unimaginable openness to foreigners from the West—specifically Americans, though many other nationalities came too—people offering help, money, and advice who normally would not be welcome. With that openness, a flood of volunteerism bathed the affected region of Chantikland. The vast majority of the longer-termed volunteers and organizations were Christian, which meant that thousands upon thousands of believers were allowed into Chantikland during that time to offer practical help and to pray with and for the Chantik.

The Venture Group recognized the ensuing influx and asked Bob to find staff to organize the short-term teams that would be coming through. It may not seem like a big deal to facilitate these teams until you realize that in just the first six months after the event forty-seven teams came to help. Each team consisted of somewhere between a handful to a dozen people, equating to well over five hundred volunteers who needed training in short order. On average, two teams were coming per week.

Bob recommended two leaders—Rizal and Rodel—for the job, and recommended that they work out of the forward operating base. Their efforts would be in tandem with Bob and Becca's. As each team arrived in-country, Bob and Becca provided the initial training at the resource

> ...thousands upon thousands of believers were allowed into Chantikland during that time.

center back in the border town of Chantikland. They educated the teams to be culturally aware, to have appropriate expectations for the devastation they would see, and to be supportive of whatever work the community organizers had negotiated with the village leaders. After training, the volunteer teams traveled to the forward operating base in Chantikland and were tactically assigned by Rizal and Rodel to work on the most current project, be it cleanup, construction, etc.

At the six-month mark, the larger international organizations started thinning out and the traffic of short-term teams shifted to the next major natural disaster in another part of the world. Teams from churches, however, just kept coming, and they did so for as long as visas were being issued. That season of intense openness only lasted between eighteen months and two years, but in that time countless Christians walked alongside the Chantik people, sharing the love of Christ through their actions and words. Believers everywhere need to pray for another season of openness among the Chantik.

A PEBBLE IN THE SEA

PRAYER #70: *"Ask God to give wisdom to Christians who will take the Good News to the Chantik, that they will be helpful in the birth of the Chantik church."*

A couple months after the disaster, and after a dozen teams had come through, Bob frequently heard a familiar statement come from the short-term teams: "We want to make an impact." Each team faithfully promised to do whatever they could to achieve that ultimate goal: *impact.* There was nothing necessarily wrong with having that as a goal, but the pressure of it weighed on Bob's heart and mind.

One morning he awoke from a restless night of sleep, even before the first call to prayer, and he called out to God, "We're small, Lord, but we want to have a big impact."

Somewhere between sleep and wakefulness the Lord showed him a vision of himself sitting in small boat, way out in the sea. The surface of the ocean around him wasn't turbulent, but it moved with the large swells of an active sea.

The Lord said, "Take a pebble out of your boat and throw it into the sea. Then, tell Me, how big of a ripple do you see?"

Tossing the pebble, Bob replied, "Lord, I don't see a ripple at all. I can't even tell that it hit the sea. The surface of the sea is rolling with movement."

"That is the impact you are going to make."

Bob thought, "Wait a second! What?"

The Lord answered his unspoken confusion. "I didn't call you to make an impact. I called you to be faithful. Don't worry about your impact. It isn't yours to make a big splash; yours is to be obedient and follow Me."

The rolling movement of the sea in Bob's dream was the movement of the Lord in His wisdom and loving-kindness. God would be the one who truly makes the impact in Chantikland, but it was the team's privilege to be present among the waves and watch it happen. With the call to be faithful still resounding in his ears, Bob roused from his waking dream and reveled in the clarity and peace he had as a result of this intimate conversation with the Lord.

Be faithful as He is faithful and let the Lord worry about the impact and outcomes of our work.

He headed to the office that morning eager to speak with the team and share his revelation. Though it was difficult for others to immediately abandon that *need* to make an impact, the call to be faithful would resonate with them in the long months of service among the Chantik. It permeated their decisions and drove their resolve to do the job they had been given, and to do it well, regardless of their size and regardless of the impact.

Bob's mantra to incoming short-term teams became "Be faithful as He is faithful and let the Lord worry about the impact and outcomes of our work." It was a freeing way to look at the work when quantifiable outcomes were slower or smaller than expected. Bob discovered that being faithful was a sustainable way to minister, whereas *achieving significant impact* was often a disappointing pursuit, with questionable biblical precedence. Being faithful to the call—*that* was his new goal moving forward in all of his ministry and outreach to the Chantik.

WHAT IS NORMAL?

PRAYER #31: *"Pray for local leaders to be open to learning the truth of Jesus Christ. Their influence could win many!"*

As the Salam Chantik project was concluding, Bob visited each village to thank the leaders for their work and to affirm that the project was finishing up. In one particular village, Bob extended fairly typical wrap-up language, albeit with genuine gratitude for the cooperation and leadership that Ismail, the village chief, had shown throughout the work in his village.

In response, Ismail just stared intently for a long time. Finally, he broke the silence and asked, "Is that it?"

"Well . . . yeah?" Bob said with a bit of confusion lacing his voice.

"There isn't anything that you want *us* to do for *you* now?"

"Ummm, no," Bob responded.

"Somewhere along the line I thought there was going to be the *big ask*," Ismail said. "I've been waiting for it."

The Chantik have a proverb that says "It is a shameful thing to be caught deceiving someone, but it is more shameful to not try." In the almost two years of the two men working together, Ismail had been trying to figure out when the other shoe was going to drop. To Ismail it was a foregone conclusion that Bob couldn't be genuine in his offer (on behalf of Salem Chantik) to help rebuild the village without wanting something back or finding some way to trick Ismail and the people. Of course this was never Bob's intention, but nevertheless when Bob responded with his final, "No, we don't need anything in return," Ismail was shocked.

A few weeks later, the central government organized a series of debriefing meetings with village leaders as the various rebuilding projects began to conclude. In one of the town hall meetings, Ismail stood up and stated, "Our village was like a wounded patient, and we were nursed back to health. Our nurse's name was Salem Chantik."

In moments like those we live out Paul's words to the Corinthians: *Thanks be to God, who always leads us as captives in Christ's triumphal procession and uses us to spread the aroma of the knowledge of him everywhere. For we are to God the pleasing aroma of Christ among those who are being saved and those who are perishing.* (2 Corinthians 2:14-15, NIV)

This was another instance of revealing how different Christ's love and generosity are than the system of suspicion and distrust that the Chantik know. Let's pray that leaders like Ismail begin to crave the smell of life and respond to Jesus with faith.

BEGINNING A NEW WORK

PRAYER #5: *"Ask God to raise up laborers who can effectively share the gospel of Jesus and disciple new believers."*

As the openness to the West, and help from foreigners (i.e., Americans), began to close down in Chantikland, the Salem Chantik projects also came to their natural conclusion. The ministry was at a turning point again. Bob and Becca had to question if they should start new initiatives or consider other paths. They turned to CHCC for guidance; and collectively, with Pastor G. and the Home Team leader, they decided that instead of starting new initiatives through Salem Chantik, which might wind up competing with local efforts by nationals, they would instead partner with those organizations and support *their* efforts.

Bob and Becca decided to return full-time to the border town. With that, they turned their attention to a variety of projects. Chief among them, for Becca, was befriending and mentoring the students at the training school. This was a wonderful opportunity to invest in the next wave of frontline workers among the Chantik. The students were from different ethnic tribes, but because they were nationals they didn't need visas to enter Chantikland.

To help them and to create more opportunities for friendship building, Becca started an English club. A number of students began coming to the club regularly to practice sharing Bible stories in English and then talking about them in English afterward. From this club Becca formed one particularly strong relationship with a girl named Tiki. She had such a passion to grow in her faith, and Becca became like a mother to her because her own mother had passed away.

Becca mentored Tiki for years, specifically through the season of life that led up to and through her first year of marriage. To continue growing both her knowledge of English and, more importantly, the depth of her faith, Becca began a special project with Tiki. Bob and Becca had provided premarriage and marriage counseling for numerous couples, often using one particular book. Becca suggested that she and Tiki work together to translate the book into the local language, and to talk about the principles as they did.

Tiki was thrilled with the idea, so together they set to work. With each chapter they translated, Tiki was so excited that she would take what she was learning back to the other nationals who were students at the church planting training school. Her enthusiasm to share meant that dozens of her colleagues learned the principles along with her. Who knows how many marriages benefited from this one mentoring project?

COMING TO YOU LIVE . . .

PRAYER #46: *"Young Chantik people love to learn the English language! Pray for the gospel to begin to be shared through relationships with English speaking Christians and media programs in English that might begin to expose the gospel."*

After the disaster, Chantikland was in chaos. Utilities were knocked out and mass communication systems were down in a number of areas. A group of Christian radio professionals saw the need and came to help. In short order, the group set up an emergency radio tower and immediately started broadcasting information about the damage, about resources available to survivors, and about where people were informally gathering to reconnect with lost family members.

The radio station started as an emergency broadcast, but after six months Chantikland began to take on more normal rhythms of life and the station thought to evolve with that shift. The Radio Group (RG)—the international parent organization of this station—was well known for its superior radio-based outreach and ministry. They took the next step and applied for a regular commercial license for an FM channel. Surprisingly, their application was approved.

With a freshly secured license to broadcast in hand, RG leadership got in contact with Bob because they needed locals to fill positions at the station on a long-term basis. Bob knew just the guy to help: an electrical engineer named Chayan, who had a wonderful combination of gifts and skills that made him an obvious candidate for station manager. RG hired Chayan immediately.

With the station manager in place—someone whom Bob already had a great working and mentoring relationship with—it was a natural step for Bob to start mentoring all of the staff. That's when Bob met Josh.

Among the international supporting organizations was an Australian NGO specializing in using radio programming to promote community and social development. The CEO of this organization, Josh, was in charge of helping the station design its programming. He trained the reporters to engage community members to hear their hearts and stories.

When Bob and Josh first met, they connected immediately. Josh had come in during the station's emergency days, and his parent organization was known for its capacity to create participatory radio programing that builds character and values into the content in culturally relevant ways as a strategic mission. This was an awesome goal in the increasingly hostile context of Chantikland.

The Chantik government was watching the station like a hawk, because the local authorities didn't like the fact that non-Chantik individuals owned the station. With that level of scrutiny, it was impossible to be an overtly Christian station and stay on the air, but with Josh's expertise and creativity they invented clever ways to expose the Chantik to gospel principles. To aid in that goal, Bob created an external foundation whose sole purpose was to create the content and provide it to the station using local issues, voices, and participation.

Though the station is still not overtly Christian, it *is* still run by Christians, and Christians still produce the content. And, with all the hard decisions they've had to make over the years, they have managed to remain ranked in the top three preferred stations out of forty in the area. With that kind of popularity we can be confident that the people are *listening*, and we as the church need to pray that they have ears to *hear* as well.

. . .

In the years following the disaster, Bob and Becca invested in national-led emerging mission initiatives, some of which included a literacy program, a local development foundation (which Bob continues to mentor even now), and a radio station. Becca's work with the students was extensive and her support to Bob unflagging.

Not surprisingly, people in and out of their organization noticed their visionary leadership and faithfulness. That notice brought with it an invitation for Bob to join the leadership team of another organization (other than the Venture Group) as the director of operations. Through extensive prayer and reflection, the Venture Group, CHCC leadership, and Bob and Becca believed this opportunity with the new organization would be a progressive step forward in their mission efforts in the region. Consequently, Bob and Becca accepted the position.

Though their Chantikland residency has ended, their work with the Chantik has not. Bob and Becca remain the overseas point people for the CHCC Home Team for that region even now and visit Chantikland several times a year. The visits allow them to check in on their colleagues and visit with friends. On a more frequent basis they stay connected to the region and the ministries through email, which allows them to continue to encourage and mentor from a distance. They have eagerly embraced the new organization and its vision to make Jesus known all the way from Northwest Africa to Southeast Asia, which includes the Chantik.

Bob and Becca are still supported by CHCC and are faithfully staying the course. They are committed to the big picture of faithfully spreading the love of Christ and letting the Lord be responsible for the impact they have.

LESSONS LEARNED

1. Don't put new wine into old wineskins—i.e., don't saddle new enthusiasm with the burdens of how the job was done in the past.
2. "Late Bloomers" can bloom beautifully.
3. Be courageous and follow the Lord, even if it is in a new and unexpected direction.
4. Our job is to be faithful; it is the Lord's job to determine the impact.

Chapter 7 Citations

1. Holy Bible. New International Version. 2 Corinthians 4:8-9.

EIGHT

A TEAM EFFORT

The LORD had said to Abram, "Go from your country, your people and your father's household to the land I will show you.

"I will make you into a great nation,
and I will bless you;
I will make your name great,
and you will be a blessing.
I will bless those who bless you,
and whoever curses you I will curse;
and all peoples on earth
will be blessed through you."
        ~Genesis 12:1-3 (NIV), The Abrahamic Covenant

All peoples on earth will be blessed through you, says the Lord in His paradigm-shifting covenant with Abraham.[1] The Lord set a precedent of how He operates in this passage of Scripture: *He blesses one, so that many will be blessed through that one.* No longer would He be a God of just one people, but of all peoples who would have Him as Lord and Savior. His heart for the nations is made clear in John 3:16-17:

For God so loved the world that he gave his one and only Son, that whoever believes in him shall not perish but have eternal life. For God did not send his Son into the world to condemn the world, but to save the world through him. We, as Christians who do claim Christ, have received that blessing and are in turn bearers of Christ's name and ambassadors on His behalf. We are now meant to be a *blessing.* That is why the gospel we bring is called the *Good News.*

Our roles as believers will vary with our spiritual gifts and the opportunities given to us by the Lord, but all who claim the name of Christ have the same call: *to be a blessing.* We do that by living out our portion of the Great Commission that Jesus gave to all believers. Taking up that charge for the last twenty-five years, CHCC (and many others) have participated in countless teams, partnerships, and creative efforts attempting to *be* that blessing to the Chantik.

BY ALL MEANS POSSIBLE

PRAYER #11: *"Pray that the Church of Jesus Christ would be established among the Chantik."*

Only our God would be so creative as to win to Himself a soul through so extravagant a scheme as the way through which one of the first, if not *the* first, modern Chantik believer came to a saving faith in Christ. He used a believer, a boat, a radio show, and a sailor. That sounds like the setup for a joke, but it's not. Our God goes to extravagant lengths to seek and save the lost; and thankfully He invites us into that process, as He did in this case.

Several decades ago, a Chantik sailor was out to sea going about his business in the Coast Guard. He happened to be sailing close enough to international waters to pick up an unusual radio broadcast. The program wasn't like anything he had ever heard before. It was in the Chantik language, so he could easily understand it, but the program was speaking about Jesus. After long hours on the sea day after day, he found himself tuning into that same broadcast.

After a time, this man understood the message of love being spoken about and had to share it. He came home and told his family what he learned from the radio broadcast, and together they chose to follow Jesus as Lord and Savior.

While the idea of a whole family making a decision for Christ is foreign to those in the West who prize individual freedom, it is as natural as can be for collectivistic cultures who value what is good for the whole over what is good for the one. In collectivistic cultures, when one believer comes to a real and saving faith, especially if he is the head of a household, he will claim, like Joshua did, "As for me and my household, we will serve the LORD."[2] Such was the case with this sailor.

Some may be skeptical about the authenticity of these group decisions, but these instances of whole groups coming to the Lord are found to have enduring depths of faith and often are the beginning of larger movements in their geographic areas referred to as *people movements*. We do know that, decades later, this sailor and his family still serve the Lord. And Jesus promises, "Where two or three gather in my name, there am I with them."[3]

This broadcast (supported by CHCC after hearing this man's story) was a brilliant effort from an organization committed to broadcasting the gospel into the hard-to-reach places of the world. They literally acquired a ship and affixed a radio tower to it, so that it could sail as close to Chantikland as possible and yet still remain in international waters. What may have appeared to some as a far-fetched plan actually turned out to be far-reaching in its impact. The program had numerous people write or call in; some were seekers with questions and others were opponents with threats.

For the years the ship operated, God's Word was being spoken in Chantik to the Chantik. And God's Word does not return void; it will accomplish what He desires and achieve the purpose for which He sent it.[4] With that in mind, let's pray that the Lord will continue to build on that which He began in one sailor and his family—and that from there, His church will be established.

PRAYING TOGETHER

PRAYER #72: *"Pray that today, and in the near future, Chantik people would gather together for fellowship with one another and worship the Lord."*

In the latter half of the 1990s, the Home Team was brimming with enthusiasm. Several successful consultations (conferences that brought together believers, churches, and mission agencies with a commitment to spreading the gospel among the Chantik) had taken place. Churches from other countries were popping up with workers ministering in and to Chantikland. And, several Go Team members were in-country, and others were about to go.

All this momentum rallied the Home Team to come up with a plan to bless both the Chantik and the missionaries sharing the gospel with them. They decided on a prayer summit, to be held in Chantikland. The plan was simple. They would encourage the believers and prayer walk through the land to pray *with* and *for* the people, as well as for missionaries—those present *and* those to come.

The goals of the prayer summit were to build up brothers and sisters in Christ and to wholeheartedly beseech the Lord on behalf of the Chantik. The summit began with the short-term team spending focused time worshiping with missionaries from four different countries, including CHCC-supported missionaries, who were there and committed to the Chantik. Then, they hit the streets, praying as they went. They wanted to consecrate the ground with their prayers, and with every step they bound up the enemy and invited the Holy Spirit to come in power.

From beginning to end, the prayer summit was an encouragement to the missionaries and believers dedicated to spreading the Good News in Chantikland. The missionaries shared that there were small pockets of believers here and there throughout the land, but they were often quite isolated from each other due to a variety of factors—the civil war, the distance, and the danger inherent in gathering a group of converts from Islam in one place. This lack of connectedness is wearing to a fledgling faith, so the missionaries asked for prayer for all who follow Christ in Chantikland, themselves included. The body of Christ could make them feel both connected and encouraged—all through the power of prayer.

A large wave of faith has yet to break on the shores of Chantikland, and the work remains hard. Pray now. Pray with conviction and persistence.

SNAP, SNAP. CLICK, CLICK.

PRAYER #15: *"For young children, ask the Lord to give them experiences of love and generosity not steeped in Islamic practice."*

PRAYER #38: *"Pray that close family ties would catalyze the spread of the gospel and not hinder it."*

Once the urgent tasks of medical care, cleanup, and community development, in the aftermath of the natural disaster, had largely been accomplished, the CHCC leaders wanted to find a special way to bless the Chantik. Working with the CHCC team in the field, particularly Becca (from chapter 7), they came up with an incredible idea to bless the Chantik by celebrating something they hold most dear—*family*.

Over what was effectively a ten-day trip, a team of ten photographers traveled from village to village, setting up large backdrops and lighting kits in the open-air community centers that act as town squares in the villages of Chantikland. Becca had worked with the community organizers to spread the word, and in each village the photographers showed up to crowded squares.

Knowing what day the photographers would come, hundreds and sometimes thousands of people greeted the team when they finally arrived. The epic crowds were filled with chatter at the extraordinary opportunity. They showed up in their finest clothing. Every child was spotless, and every elder was transported to the center of the village for the event. There was so much joy that even the long hours of waiting in line were redeemed by the chance it afforded neighbors to talk and laugh, to share carefree time with each other, and to catch up without their attention being demanded elsewhere.

The process for each family was simple. They would show up for their family photo in the morning (or afternoon), and the next morning (or afternoon) the team would return with an 8 x 10 color photo of that family, which was framed and under glass. Each family received their framed portrait as a free gift. The Chantik had endured such a devastating loss of life during the natural disaster that this gift, which honored the family members who had survived, was precious to them.

The process for the team was anything but simple. Fortunately, Becca had done the heavy lifting of preparing the villages for the events, outlining a rigorous schedule that the team would have to keep, and sourcing local vendors who could print the photos and make the frames. All that preparation allowed the photographers to focus on their task. When the A group went out in the morning to photograph, the B group's cameras were charging and they were pulling the photos from the memory cards from their last session to get them developed. In the afternoons, the roles were reversed. Both groups worked tirelessly to take the photos, get them developed, and then frame them all before delivering them to the families the very next day!

All in all, this one short-term team shot, developed, framed, and delivered *1,100 portraits.* That's right, 1,100! The families varied in size from two to twelve (and sometimes more). Collectively, thousands of Chantik people were blessed by this outreach—and that kind of blessing bears fruit.

About four years later, another short-term team from CHCC went back to some of the villages where the portraits had been taken. Ellis, who went on both trips, ran into a man whom he had photographed earlier. Recognizing each other, they began talking at length. The Chantik man was so excited to see Ellis that he ran to his home to get both his daughter and the original photograph that Ellis took. It was still beautifully framed, and revealed how much his young daughter had grown. The original gift still held such goodwill, even years later, that the men talked and talked. They ended their time by Ellis taking an updated shot of the man and his daughter, so that he could remember them both in prayer.

This gesture of kindness and generosity was intended to be a blessing to the Chantik, and it *was*. Additionally, those 1,100 families bore witness to Christians showing the love and generosity of our Savior, Jesus Christ, through their words and deeds. That prepares the ground for seeds sown in the future. In fact, we pray that the blessing of that trip will continue to have ripple effects of goodwill for any missionary who comes in the name of Christ to those villages.

TWICE OVER

PRAYER #66: *"God desires all men to be saved. Ask Him for the salvation of the Chantik!"*

Because the portrait trip was such a well-greased machine of organization (which it had to be to get the right photo into the hands of the right family), that made the next step a no-brainer. The short-term team came home with the all the information they needed for an eternally valuable second-wave effort to bless the Chantik, and they got right on it.

In the process of taking the photos, the team wrote down the names of every family member in every single photo. Within weeks of their trip, they printed up and distributed 1,100 prayer cards— with a photo of each family and the name of each person pictured on each card.

Small groups and individuals, pastors and laypeople took the cards. In fact, CCHC members came out of the woodwork until all the cards had been distributed. This wave of prayer for the Chantik happened thirteen years after the initial prayer guide was published (i.e., the guide containing the prayers found throughout this book).

Oh Lord, hear our prayers, both then and now.

· · ·

The Holy Spirit is moving around the world, and the ripples of His movement have created waves of prayer among His servants over the twenty-five years of work with the Chantik. From the first wave, with two twenty-somethings who sparked CHCC to seek the Lord's direction about adopting the Chantik, to the consultations in the United States and the conference held in the border town to Chantikland, to the prayer summit a few years later, to the portrait prayer cards a few years ago. It seems we are due for another major wave of prayer that leads us back to being a blessing to the Chantik.

Chapter 8 Citations

1. Holy Bible. New International Version. Genesis 12:1-3.
2. Holy Bible. New International Version. Joshua 24:15b.
3. Holy Bible. New International Version. Matthew 18:20.
4. Holy Bible. New King James Version. Isaiah 55:11.

NINE

A 25-YEAR SNAPSHOT

Expect great things from God. Attempt great things for God.
~ William Carey, 1792
(Known as the first Protestant missionary
to India and the father of modern missions)

J esus gave us the task: To "go and make disciples of all
nations, baptizing them in the name of the Father and of the Son
and of the Holy Spirit, and teaching them to obey everything I have
commanded you" (Matthew 28:19-20). And the apostle Paul made
the mode of accomplishing the task clear: we must act boldly on
behalf of the gospel to share the Good News with many, "so that
by all possible means [we] might save some" (1 Corinthians 9:22).

Nothing about this unique chapter is meant to be a pat on the
back to CHCC alone. In fact, sharing the following statistics has
the sole purpose of giving a glimpse of the mighty work being done
by THE CHURCH. These statistics just happen to be those which
were confirmed through the work of or in coordination with the Go
Team members—Tim, Sandy, Gwen, Kathy, Bob and Becca—and
the long-term missionary partners, James and Ayu. These details
are but a tiny fraction of the whole work being done. These figures

should inspire you to pray for the ongoing efforts and the ones that have yet to be attempted.

Through dozens of churches, organizations, and mission agencies and tens of thousands of individual believers, the Holy Spirit has worked and is working. Notably, the Spirit started moving in the hearts of His servants on behalf of the Chantik nearly four decades ago, and the rubber began to meet the road twenty-five years ago. Since that time, innumerable efforts have been made to spread the gospel in Chantikland.

The hymn "The Love of God" by Frederick M. Lehman written in 1917 captured an appropriate level of awe when he shared that even if the ocean was ink and the sky itself a scroll, there still would not be enough room to record the love of the Lord or the miracles He has worked. However, to give our awe a focus, the following figures are a snapshot of God's great work among the Chantik over the last twenty-five years.

• • •

STATS

OF

EVENTS

```
##
####
######
########
```

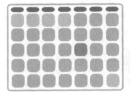

1 PRAYER SUMMIT
IN CHANTIKLAND
WITH 4 COUNTRIES
SENDING PARTICIPANTS

1 CIVIL WAR

6 CONSULTATIONS
WHERE **100s** GATHER'D TO COMMIT TO **THE CHANTIK**

1 CHRISTIAN CONFERENCE
IN CHANTIKLAND'S NATION
WITH **400** **NATIONAL LEADERS**
COMMITTED TO FOCUSED OUTREACH
TO CHANTIKLAND

1 NATURAL DISASTER
WHICH KILLED 5% OF THE POPULATION
IN TEN HORRIBLE MINUTES

STATS OF SHORT-TERM WORK

24 SHORT-TERM CHCC TRIPS IN 25 YEARS

OVER **200** SHORT-TERM CHCC TEAM MEMBERS HAVE GONE TO **CHANTIKLAND**

PASTORAL 13 VISITS

STATS OF
LONG-TERM WORKERS

10 LONG-TERM
MISSIONARIES
MOBILIZED THRU CHCC

150 YEARS
OF COLLECTIVE SERVICE FROM THE EIGHT
LONG-TERM WORKERS IN THIS BOOK

40 + **PRAYER WARRIORS**
ON THE HOME TEAM

HUNDREDS
OF **NATIONAL**
CHURCH PLANTERS
MOBILIZED

STATS OF COLLABORATION

CHURCHES FROM **5** CONTINENTS SERVING **CHANTIKLAND**

THE COLLABORATIVE EFFORT

3 MEGA CHURCHES

DOZENS OF SMALLER **CHURCHES**

12+ DENOMINATIONS **WORKING TOGETHER**

DOZENS OF **NGOs**

HALF DOZEN MISSION AGENCIES COLLABORATING

47 SHORT-TERM TEAMS FROM PARTNERS IN **SIX** MONTHS **AFTER THE DISASTER**

DURING THE CIVIL WAR

STATS OF TANGIBLES

\#\# \#\#\#\#

1000s OF CIVIL WAR REFUGEES FED

HUNDREDS of CHICKENS

DRIVEN IN TO THE **WAR ZONE** BY VAN TO FEED **REFUGEES** HIDING IN MOSQUES FROM THE CIVIL WAR

1000s of Chantik learned English

as a result of our missionaries teaching English to hundreds of Chantik teachers

1 CARGO CONTAINER OF FOOD STUFFS & MEDICAL SUPPLIES FOR REFUGEES

STATS OF TANGIBLES

AFTER THE NATURAL DISASTER

####

1200

49,000 PEOPLE
GIVEN MEDICAL CARE
IN 6 WEEKS AFTER THE DISASTER

micro finance

loans & grants

3900 HOMES
BUILT or REPAIRED
over five years

Tons upon Tons
MEDICAL SUPPLIES
DISTRIBUTED

500
illustrated
books on hygiene
created & distributed

STATS OF **TANGIBLES** ## ####

1 BIRTHING CENTER BUILT

60+ babies BORN AT THE BIRTHING CENTER WITHIN WEEKS OF THE DISASTER

2 BOAT WORKS BUILT

*a boat works is a company that builds boats

1100 CHANTIK FAMILIES HAD THEIR PORTRAIT TAKEN, PRINTED, FRAMED & GIVEN TO THEM AS A GIFT AFTER THE NATURAL DISASTER

THE PORTRAITS WERE TURNED INTO **1100 PRAYER CARDS** WITH NAMES AND DISTRIBUTED TO CHCC FAMILIES TO PRAY FOR THEM SPECIFICALLY.

PRAYER CARDS

OVER THE YEARS

STATS OF TANGIBLES ## ####

3 RADIO STATIONS SUPPORTED

1000s RADIO SEGMENTS
PRODUCED (INCLUDING BIBLE-BASED,
CULTURALLY RELEVANT SHOWS, AND
DIRECT GOSPEL PREACHING)

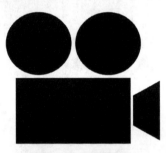

**JESUS FILM
TRANSLATED**
INTO CHANTIK

NEW TESTAMENT
TRANSLATED INTO
THE CHANTIK LANGUAGE

• 100s • 100s • 100s •
OF BIBLES GIVEN AWAY

TEN

CALLING YOU TO ACTION

Only the Master knows exactly what
He wants each servant to do.

~ T. Wayne Dye[1]

God is constantly working toward the fulfillment of His will—His good, pleasing, and perfect will.[2] And, because of His great love for us, He gives our lives purpose as individuals—each with good deeds prepared in advance for us to do[3]—and as the church, to be His ambassadors.[4] So when we've been given a task or a calling, why then do we waver from it?

When we've been called to some work—individually and/or collectively—let us not grow weary in doing good. The Lord promises that we will reap fruit from our labors, in due season, if we do not lose heart.[5] It is to this end that we must press on.

Faithful And Flexible

The first critical step of obedience in our calling is trusting the Lord and recognizing His responsibility for the results of our labor. We are sowers of seeds—doing good work—but He is the one who will produce the growth. He is the one who will determine if that seed will produce a crop of a hundred, sixty, or thirty times what was sown.[6] He is the maker of the seasons and knows when the time has come for each and every good work to move from seed to sprout, sprout to sapling, sapling to mighty oak. He guides our hands as we plant; our job is to be faithful to the calling and trust Him with the rest.

The second requisite of wisdom in calling is knowing how to be faithful and yet remain flexible. A God-given calling should remain one's mantle until He removes it; however, the approach to accomplish the task may constantly be revisited. Why labor vainly in one direction when another may prove more effective, more efficient, or simply better? Every great endeavor should be able to bear the scrutiny of an evaluation without that process throwing into question the validity of the calling itself.

It's Your Turn

CHCC is a real church, partnering in real ways with the Lord as He moves in the world. The Chantik are equally real. However, both CHCC and the Chantik are representational of *the church* and *all people* who have yet to hear the gospel message. There is still work to be done, as Jesus summed up in Matthew 9 when He said, "The harvest is plentiful, but the workers are few."[7]

Whether your story is wrapped up in the Chantik people and the work being done there, or some other people group or passion, the question becomes, *What is God calling you to next?* What missional step will you take to be—or to remain—faithful to what God has called you to?

After reading about this prayer movement and seeing all of the big and little ways that the Lord has answered prayers, what is He stirring in your heart? This may be the moment when you receive clear direction, and you need to be bold in taking a step forward in that call. Boldness could look like any number of things. It could mean joining a prayer movement that is already happening, as with the Chantik, and fulfilling Jesus' next thought in the Matthew 9 passage: "Therefore beseech the Lord of the harvest to send out workers into His harvest."[8] It could mean learning more about missions or finding an agency and going on the field with the support of your sending church. Only you and the Lord know what that next step might be.

If you don't have a clear direction forward at this moment, then seek the Lord in prayer first and foremost. Ask for clarity, and be patient as you listen. If waiting isn't the easiest thing for you, then be wise and use the time to make yourself an even more useful tool for the Lord by getting training from experts and practitioners. Meeting with a pastor or missionary is an easy first step. Maybe you could take a class at a seminary or find a local session of the Perspectives class that Kathy took (see chapter 5). Perspectives on the World Christian Movement classes are held throughout the year, in hundreds of locations across the United States, in a number of countries around the world, and online. The class was designed by the U.S. Center for World Mission, now called Frontier Ventures, and is a comprehensive course for anyone seeking advancement in their knowledge and resources regarding God's heart for the nations. The point is to seek the Lord and let Him direct your path.

Perhaps you don't feel called to a current prayer movement, but you feel like the Lord is challenging you to start one where there hasn't been one. If so, that is wonderful. According to research generated from Finishing the Task—an association of mission agencies and churches that gathers statistics about people groups—there were roughly 3,000 unengaged people groups around the world as of 2015.[9]

If you are meant to start something, then God is most certainly stirring in the hearts of other believers as well. Start sharing the idea around in the community of believers you are connected with and see if the Holy Spirit is stirring anyone in the same way to come alongside of you. Catherine and Darren (from chapter 2) would have been written off by a lot of people as "just twenty-somethings", but they came back from their first trip and started the conversation of adoption about the Chantik with CHCC. It was confirmation to their calling to see that the Lord was most certainly moving in the hearts of the leadership who responded with enthusiasm to their passionate vision.

Over the years, thousands and thousands of people have been mobilized to pray for, go to, and share the love of Christ with the Chantik. If the Lord gives you a calling, it is your responsibility to follow Him with firm resolve and remain faithful as you wait to see what He will make of your work.

Don't Expect It To Be Easy

The current leader of the Chantik Home Team, Perry, put it well when he said, "This new generation is willing to do good things, but it remains to be seen whether they are willing to do something hard, and missions in places like Chantikland is hard." He described the work as the back-breaking, heart-wrenching work of "tilling the soil so that it will be ready for the seeds when they are planted."

Whether we are talking about bringing the gospel to unreached peoples like the Chantik or working on big issues like ending human trafficking, the work is hard and the task is long. Perry went on to say, "It is noteworthy that we've stayed in the race. We haven't always been running, but we have stayed in the race. It has been a relay race, and the truth of the matter is that in our frailties as humans we need it to be a relay, because no one can carry the weight of that work for a lifetime."

Ron Sider, a theologian and social activist, asserts that "Nobody can do everything, but everybody can do something, and together we can change the world."[10] You know you have a calling. The Lord gives each one of us gifts and passion. The final question becomes, *What is your role in the grand scheme of God's will and what are you going to do about it?*

Chapter 10 Citations

1. T. Wayne Dye, "Discovering the Holy Spirit's Work in a Community," in Ralph D. Winter, *Perspectives on the World Christian Movement: A Reader* (4th ed., 2014). Pasadena, CA: William Carey Library.
2. Holy Bible. New International Version. Romans 12:2.
3. Holy Bible. New International Version. Ephesians 2:10.
4. Holy Bible. New International Version. 2 Corinthians 5:20.
5. Holy Bible. New International Version. Galatians 6:9.
6. Holy Bible. New International Version. Matthew 13:8.
7. Holy Bible. New American Standard Bible. Matthew 9:37.
8. Holy Bible. New American Standard Bible. Matthew 9:38.
9. "About Finishing the Task." Finishing the Task website. Accessed February 3, 2015. http://www.finishingthetask.com/about.html.
10. Ron Sider, "State of World Need," in Ralph D. Winter, *Perspectives on the World Christian Movement: A Reader* (4th ed., 1981). Pasadena, CA: William Carey Library.

NEXT STEPS

OPPORTUNITIES TO LEARN:

- Learn about God's heart for the nations by taking the Perspectives on the World Christian Movement class at www.perspectives.org. Classes are held regularly all over the country (and world) and likely at a church near you.
- Read a missionary biography or mission-themed book. (Go to www. dgwynn.com and under "Resources" you'll find my "Recommended Reading Lists" by missional topic/focus.)

OPPORTUNITIES TO PRAY:

- Download the Joshua Project app (or go to www.joshuaproject.net) to pray for a different unreached people group each day.
- Find out what missionaries your church supports and pray for them and the people they minister among.

OPPORTUNITIES TO SEND:

Lack of support is one of the top three reasons missionaries have to leave the field. They need both prayer and funds to do the work. Both are valuable.

- Support a missionary from your church.
- Support a missionary you've met.
- Support a missionary through a project that you are passionate about.
- Support a mission project.
- Support a mission agency.

- Support a student who is intending to be a missionary.
- Support an international student's dream to attend seminary, so they can bring deeper learning back to their people when they are finished studying.

OPPORTUNITIES TO GO:

- Go to your pastor and seek out short-term and long-term opportunities to do missions.
- See if your denomination has a missions agency.
- Attend missions conferences like:
  - o Urbana - www.urbana.org
  - o Missio Nexus – www.missionexus.org
- See what kind of local outreach opportunities are in your city, in your neighborhood, in your church.
- Walk across the driveway or parking lot and get to know your neighbor.

Perspectives
on the World Christian Movement™

WHAT IS PERSPECTIVES?

PERSPECTIVES is a 15-week class designed around four vantage points or "perspectives" — Biblical, Historical, Cultural and Strategic. Each one highlights different aspects of God's global purpose. The Perspectives course will deepen your knowledge of God's heart for the nations and challenge you in new ways to be part of His movement in the world.

PERSPECTIVES IS FOR BELIEVERS FROM ALL WALKS OF LIFE:
Professionals, business leaders, high school students, college students, military personnel, pastors, missionaries on the field and those preparing for the field, mission leadership, retirees, and many others.

Perspectives is a ministry of Frontier Ventures, formerly the US Center for World Mission, a nondenominational ministry serving churches and mission agencies worldwide.

Call 888-777-3806, email info@perspectives.org or go to www.perspectives.org to learn more.

LIST OF ORIGINAL PRAYERS

Here are the original seventy-two prayers listed in the Chantik Prayer Guide written nearly twenty-five years ago. There is nothing perfect about this list. It was written by men and women whose perspectives and paradigms colored the wording and nature of each prayer. Nonetheless, it is an excellent example of a valiant effort to lead others in prayer for a particular unreached people group.

[Those in **bold** are prayers which were fulfilled in part, in full, or for a time as recounted in this book.]

1. **Pray for the government—continued openness to American business and American people. Pray for willingness to equally protect the rights of the less-populous Christians in their mostly Muslim country.**

2. **Pray for media to contain more Christian values for the Chantik. Ask for their discernment to filter out sensational and immoral programming.**

3. **Pray for Christians to be willing to step through the open door for English language teachers to the Chantik.**

4. **Pray for the basic needs of the Chantik to be met: health care, dental care, sanitation.**

5. **Ask God to raise up laborers who can effectively share the gospel of Jesus and disciple new believers.**

6. Ask that the Chantik be freed from Islam, which effectively keeps them from hearing the truth about Jesus Christ.

7. Pray for the Chantik people to see that you cannot reach God through mere human effort.

8. Pray that God would bind the spiritual forces of Islam, which keep people from the truth.

9. **God longs for the Chantik people to know Him. Pray that those who seek God will find Him, whether that be through dreams or visions or the testimony of believers.**

10. **Pray that the Chantik people would know Jesus as their only Hope and Savior.**

11. **Pray that the church of Jesus Christ would be established among the Chantik.**

12. **Pray that the Chantik people would know the truth, and that the truth would set them free.**

13. **Pray for many Muslims to honestly face the questions they have about Islam (e.g., Why after fasting for the month of Ramadan can you still have evil or hateful thoughts about others if the fasting was supposed to purify your heart?). Pray they would find the answer to these questions in Jesus' cleansing blood.**

14. Pray for the young people who are beginning to understand more of the meaning behind Ramadan. Ask the Father to open their eyes to the futility of earning salvation.

15. **For young children, ask the Lord to give them experiences of love and generosity not steeped in Islamic practice.**

16. Thank God for the strength than can be built in family relationships through visiting and sharing of a special time together. May these family ties be stronger than commitment to Islam.

17. Pray that the imams' messages during the month of Ramadan would not have the desired results of motivating people toward legalistic pride. May they unintentionally expose the insufficiency of human effort.

18. **Praise the Lord for His searching love, which extends to every human being. May He redeem the desires of Muslims who are honestly pursuing the Truth. Ask for their fasting and searching to be met with the truth of Jesus Christ.**

19. **Ask the Lord of the harvest to send laborers to the Chantik—that they may know Jesus and then influence many ethnic groups.**

20. Thank God for assembling different ethnic peoples in the capital city and for the opportunity to influence other peoples from that starting point.

21. Ask God to raise up influential Muslim converts who can return to their place of origin to report that they have met the Savior.

22. Praise God for the friendships in the capital city that cross ethnic lines. Pray for this favor to continue so that God might bless the "nations" through the Chantik.

23. Pray particularly for university students who come to the capital from many different regions and ethnic groups.

24. Pray that the future Chantik church would have vision to share the gospel with other Muslim peoples.

25. Thank the Lord for the strong, family orientation in the village communities. Pray, though, for openness to new ideas and willingness to accept family members who are first to accept Christ.

26. Pray for great courage for new Christians. They will possibly face rejection and persecution from families and village communities.

27. Pray for community-building traditions, which are not strictly Islamic, to gain popularity.

28. Pray for favor and acceptance for Christian workers in these tightly knit, same-thinking communities.

29. Pray for imams and other community leaders to govern diligently and faithfully, putting the good of their people above their own good.

30. Pray for village leaders to know the salvation of Christ and use their great influence for His Kingdom.

31. Pray for local leaders to be open to learning the truth of Jesus Christ. Their influence could win many!

32. Pray against the strongholds of pride and legalism built up through a thick system of religious laws.

33. Ask that Chantik leaders would truly care for their people and be used by God to provide Godly advice.

34. Pray that Christians who go among the Chantik could find favor in the eyes of local leaders.

35. Ask for God's choice of future leaders to be put in place, whose lives can serve to advance His Kingdom.

36. **Pray for the men who will one day be leaders among the Chantik. May they hear and respond to the gospel at the proper time in their lives.**

37. Pray that God would prepare the hearts of Chantik family heads to receive the Good News of Jesus.

38. **Pray that close family ties would catalyze the spread of the gospel and not hinder it.**

39. **Pray for Chantik fathers—that God would prepare their hearts to receive the gospel. Pray that they would have courage to embrace Christ and that their families would follow.**

40. **Pray for fathers' relationships with their families. These men could be a light to their village communities and extended family in the way they love their families. Ask God to work a radical transformation in their hearts.**

41. Pray for Chantik mothers. They have closer relationships with their children than fathers do. Ask that God would include many Chantik mothers in His Kingdom and that the mothers would influence their children for good.

42. Pray for extended family relations. Grandparents and elderly people own a special degree of honor, and they have power to influence their families for good or for evil. Pray that older people would embrace the Lord Jesus Christ.

43. Pray for the younger generation who are being influenced by modern music and television—that they would be protected from the immoral influence of the media, yet have the courage to learn new things and challenge their faith in Islam.

44. **Pray for teachers in high schools and universities—that the influence they have on the younger generation might be redeemed and used by God to reveal His truth.**

45. Pray for a student movement, where the younger generation might worship the Lord together on their campuses and in their neighborhoods.

46. **Young Chantik people love to learn the English language! Pray for the gospel to begin to be shared through relationships with English speaking Christians and media programs in English that might begin to expose the gospel.**

47. **As the younger generations struggle with finding their own identity, pray they would find it in the Lord Jesus Christ.**

48. As new interests and values conflict with old ones, pray that the younger generation will treasure the beautiful things of their culture while keeping up with the modernization of the West.

49. **Pray that God would raise up Christians who desire to share the gospel of Jesus while teaching English to avid, Chantik learners.**

50. **Pray that God would raise up Christians with skills in community development work (computer education, agriculture, sanitation, health, dental, and urban planning) to serve the Chantik people tangibly as well as eternally.**

51. **As the Chantik people desire to emulate the West, pray they only emulate what is helpful for a developing country and reject that which is ungodly.**

52. Pray that God would open up many other opportunities in which foreign Christians can have holistic ministries among the Chantik.

53. Pray that the Chantiks' interest in receiving help from the West will remain positive and open.

54. **Long-term visas are necessary in order to live and work among the Chantik. Pray that the process of obtaining visas from the Chantik government will be easy and smooth.**

55. Pray that the poor among the Chantik would soon know and understand the gospel of Jesus Christ.

56. Pray against the fatalistic attitude, which some poor Chantik men have. Pray that they will have the courage to help their families out of poverty.

57. **Pray for openings for poor Chantik people to gain good employment, even if they have no rich connections.**

58. **Pray that God would raise up Christians who would be willing to serve and reach out to the Chantik poor.**

59. Pray for the future Chantik church to powerfully minister to the poor in their cities and villages.

60. **Pray against the resignation to spiritual nonunderstanding and spiritual poverty, which is so common among the Muslim Chantik. Ask for the Holy Spirit to stir them with a hunger to know the truth through questioning Islam.**

61. **Pray for the devil's schemes to be thwarted so that the minds of the Chantik Muslims will see the "light of the gospel that displays the glory of Christ, who is the image of God."**

62. Pray for Chantiks to realize that they can become followers of Jesus without abandoning their own cultural identity.

63. **Pray that Chantik Muslims will test Islam to see if it is really from God.**

64. **Pray for missionaries to effectively share the gospel with Chantik Muslims.**

65. Pray that the Holy Spirit will convict Chantik Muslims of their guilt and that they would turn to Jesus, the only One who can take away that guilt.

66. **God desires all men to be saved. Ask Him for the salvation of Chantik Muslims!**

67. **God knows the future for the Chantik church, which will be established one day. Pray for His will to be done.**

68. **Pray that God would call to Himself men who are leaders in their families and communities, that those who presently teach Islam would teach salvation by faith in Christ instead.**

69. Pray that God would give courage and strength, hope and faith, to those who are among the first Chantik people to follow Jesus.

70. **Ask God to give wisdom to Christians who will take the Good News to the Chantik, that they will be helpful in the birth of the Chantik church.**

71. Ask God to use people who come to Christ in the Chantik capital to take the Good News back to their home villages.

72. **Pray that today, and in the near future, Chantik people would gather together for fellowship with one another and worship the Lord.**

ACKNOWLEDGEMENTS

A few years ago the Lord got my attention in a significant way and forced me to examine my life, to really figure out what I wanted to be when I grew up. True, that's an odd conversation to be having in my 30s, when I was very busy as an adjunct professor and highly involved in my church and local groups, but He started a conversation of thought in my head that I couldn't ignore.

I became obsessed with the concept of *trajectory* and how all the little decisions we make now will influence where we wind up as we travel down the path of life. Piece by piece I examined my life and asked, "Where is that headed?" and "Is _____ going to end up in 40 years somewhere I'll be happy about?"

For the first time in, well *ever*, I was willing to scrap it all, take a sabbatical and figure out what I wanted to be about for the rest of my life. However, because I'm not independently wealthy, it was clear that I needed to work while I was figuring it out. It was equally clear that I couldn't continue doing the all-consuming university work that I had been letting fill up the years. (Grading is a mind-numbing activity even when you love your subject. Kiss the next teacher you see and just say 'thank you' for the sacrifice their work entails.)

In my quest to "figure it out" I reached out to several dozen CEOs and nonprofit leaders in Denver whom I knew and took meetings with all of them saying the same thing, "I can write and I can edit, do you have any work for me?"

Surprisingly, one of the first meetings I took was with Pastor G. of this book. He said, "I have a writing project for you," and after a thirty-minute conversation I asked, "Do you mean you want me to write a book?" And long story short, the first steps down the path to a lot of research, writing, and joyful toil began that day.

I'll forever be thankful for that first meeting because it led me to write this book, which allowed me to tell the story of so many amazing people, not to mention just hinting at some of the amazing work the Lord is doing around the world.

In the last three years, I figured out that writing is where I find deep joy, not just satisfaction or accomplishment, but *joy*. Like Eric Liddell, the Olympic runner, who felt God's pleasure when he ran, I feel it when I write. And what a privilege it is to write about God's people doing things to bring Him glory. I may never be rich, but I am most certainly blessed, and that is an outcome I can live with.

While that is the short version of what led me to write this book, I have a million people to thank for helping me keep on keeping on. (Not everything is roses and sunshine, even when you find joy in your work!)

To that end, I want to say thanks to you all.

THANK YOU to my mom—my chief supporter and dearest friend, the cooker of meals and keeper of my sanity, my traveling buddy and the woman I aspire to be. Thank you for your unwavering love, especially when I least deserve it.

THANK YOU to my dad for inspiring me, teaching me, encouraging me to dream big and in many ways for shaping me into the person that I am today. I miss you.

THANK YOU to my family—Chris, Kara, Mason, Sawyer, Hondo, Trisha, Caleb, and Elizabeth, and to all my cousins, aunts and uncles—for their love and support.

THANK YOU to my best friends—Kirsten, Mindi, Naisa and Trip— you've always celebrated and cherished the weirdness that is me, and been there for me through all of my ups and downs. Thank you for letting me experience the fullest and most pure expression of friendship in your love.

THANK YOU to my beta readers and friends who have encouraged me and spurred me on in my writing: Taya Johnson, Chris Horst, Harold Britton, Georges Houssney, Andy Sloan, Rachel and Chris Tyrrell, John Lites, Ryan Hale, Leonie Kent, Dr. John Stebbins, Riker Johnson, Moses and Jaime Okonji, and Collins Sande.

THANK YOU to the team of people from CHCC who not only are the subject of this book, but the entire reason it was possible to write and eventually publish it. This team sacrificed their time, talent, and resources countless times to make this book a reality. Believe me when I tell you that a million prayers were offered and answered in the making of this book! Praise God for His faithfulness in long hard tasks.

THANK YOU to Pastor G. for his leadership and to CHCC for the 25 years of collective effort to glorify the Lord and expand His Kingdom. I think we are all excited to see what the next 25 years holds.

And last but not least, I THANK THE LORD for His grace and love. Words are too small to express all that is in my heart.

ABOUT THE AUTHOR

D.G. Wynn was a missionary with CRM (Church Resource Ministries) and worked side-by-side with Navigators in Glasgow, Scotland. Since her return from the field she's been a passionate missions advocate working in the local church and missions community of Denver, CO.

She's been involved in short-term missions for almost 20 years and is a staunch advocate of church-wide prayer being key to prosperous ministry locally and internationally. D.G. partnered with Cherry Hills Community Church and their outreach department to help tell this story of the work among the Chantik and inspire the next generation of missionaries—those who go across the world and those who go across the street.

While "The Prayers of Many" was her first published book, it will by no means be the last. Look for her next book out in early 2017, it's called "Mission-Wise: The Compact Guide to Before, During, and After Your Short-term Trip". It was written to improve the experience of short-term missionaries and their efficacy in the field and afterward.

In addition to promoting missions and prayer through her writing, she is a national speaker with the Perspectives on the World Christian Movement and speaks regularly at conferences, events, and schools.

Connect with her at www.dgwynn.com or on facebook by searching 'D.G. Wynn' or on Twitter @DG_Wynn.